And God blessed them, say
fill the waters in the seas, and

Genesis 1:22

Long Tailed Fowl

Their History and Care

by

David Rogers and Toni-Marie Astin

ISBN 10: 1-57472-414-2
ISBN 13: 978-1-57472-414-1

Edited by Julia Keeling and Marc King

Printed in the U.S.A.

Cover photos by David Rogers.

Front cover - Black-breasted red long tailed rooster - Rogers line.

Back cover ;
Top left - Gold duckwing bantam Phoenix hen - Rogers line.
Bottom - Silver duckwing Ohiki rooster - Astin line.

Introduction

In Japan, the home of long tailed fowl, there are six different long tailed breeds: Totenko, Shokoku, Minohiki, Ohiki, Kurokashiwa and Onagadori.

Phoenix and Yokohama were developed from these breeds in Europe; there are no breeds of these names in Japan.

The main purposes of this book are -

- to help enthusiasts who wish to develop the original type and characteristics of the Onagadori, the fabulous breed of Kochi (Tosa) with the non-molting tail reaching lengths of thirty feet plus;
- to clarify that Onagadori and Phoenix are not the same breed;
- to provide information on the care and requirements of long tailed fowl.

It is not a comprehensive compilation of information on all these breeds but is designed to help breeders become better informed, to decide if long tailed breeds are right for them, and to provide basic information regarding the background, genetics, and care of long tailed breeds.

The authors would like to note that, at the time of this writing, pure Onagadori are not available in the US or in most other countries outside of Japan.

Contents

Breed History and Development of the Japanese Onagadori, 尾長鶏

Other breeds outside Japan, such as Phoenix and Yokohama, have been mistakenly called “Onagadori”, but the Onagadori is a specific breed, distinct from any other. It becomes obvious that no other breed of fowl can claim to the name when it is clearly understood what an Onagadori is: the possessor of a unique genetic makeup which causes the males of the breed to go without molting certain groups of tail feathers for years at a time when given the correct environment.

The breed is thought to have originated from a mixture of Red and Green Jungle Fowl, inheriting some traits from each ancestor. To this day there is a breed in Java called the Bekisar that is a hybrid of a male Green Jungle Fowl and Red Jungle Fowl hen. The resulting male offspring is usually sterile. However, occasionally a partially fertile male will be produced. These hybrids carry the tail genes of the Onagadori, as well as the long-crowing gene of breeds like the Tomaru, Denizli, Totenko, and Koeyoshi. The latter two breeds are not known to exist in the United States at the time of writing.

One might imagine from this present-day hybrid how the Onagadori could have been produced in the breed’s early days of development prior to it being homozygous for its best-known traits.

The Onagadori was not just another ‘pretty face’ bred purely to look attractive. It had a purpose long ago in Tosa, now modern day Kochi, where it was developed. It is said that farmers who raised the fowl would use the tail feathers as a form of tax payment to the prefectural Shogun’s regional Daimyo during Japan’s feudal period. These breeders were then exempt from paying monetary taxes. The feathers were used to adorn the ceremonial spears and helmets of these military officials. This ornamentation made the Tosa procession instantly recognizable.

The tails were not always the length that they are today. The trait started out simply with a few birds that had slightly longer than

normal tails, perhaps only two or three feet in length. Through selective breeding, and a high level of care from their keepers, the tails attained greater lengths over time. A few centuries later tails of nine feet or more were becoming more common.

Left - Artifacts from the feudal period in Japan's past on display at a museum in Kochi, Japan. In the foreground is a ceremonial warrior helmet decorated with feathers of long tailed fowl. In the background, a feather covered decoration for atop a large staff. Photo courtesy of Julia Keeling.

In the early 1920s some breeders began to use special cages for the roosters. The same style of cage is still in use today. The Japanese breeders call these cages tomebako, or "stopping box". The name "stopping box" comes about due to the practice of using the box to keep the rooster calm, keep its hormones from fluctuating, and thereby suppressing the regular molt pattern of the tail coverts, sickles, and saddle feathers, which usually occurs every one to two years. Nevertheless, some 20% to 40% of these feathers may still molt on even the best quality Onagadori. The main tail feathers are of an extreme length compared to other breeds, but they molt regularly unlike the coverts, sickles, and saddles.

Once tomebako were implemented, tail lengths of twenty feet and more in length were appearing in flocks of more refined birds. Tail length continued in this way until the 1970s.

It was near this same point in time that health, vigor, disease resistance, and life span diminished in some lines. It has been debated by various people why the breed has gone into a decline. Some say that it is due to inbreeding, others say that they were always weak to some degree.

Any time a hybrid of two species is made there is potential

for the cross to either not work, or to do so for only for a short time. The key to reviving such a cross is to select for the traits of one of the ancestors. Since the Red Jungle Fowl does not carry the required genes for long tailed breeds, it would be essential to reselect for those genetics from the Green Jungle Fowl ancestor.

It would potentially prove beneficial to take a step back and reintroduce new blood, in the form of a Green Jungle Fowl, to any long tailed line that is weakening. Using birds that look most like a pure-bred example and which exhibit the best feather traits for breeding back to pure stock would soon produce birds as they were, nearer to the original healthier line of long ago.

As for the claim that the tail genes cause a weakness, this could be true to an extent. However, the fact that the breed did flourish at one time suggests that this is not necessarily the case. Looking over the possible origin of the Onagadori and the likelihood of it containing heavy concentrations of Green Jungle Fowl genetics, breeders of the Onagadori should consider how wild Green Jungle Fowl are kept in captivity.

Jungle Fowl are not from a cold climate, living as they do in jungles and forests in subtropical to warm temperate areas throughout Asia. In the United States, the closest climate to that of Kochi, Japan, is the region around Chesapeake Bay in Virginia. If a life form develops in a specific climate, it will not easily acclimatize to a different climate. Green Jungle Fowl must be kept warm in captivity to simulate their natural environment - at least above 50°F in the winter. The breed is simply not cold tolerant.

Most poultry breeders cannot easily heat an entire flock. So if the cold temperatures of the northern climates are a factor in long tailed fowl not doing well in those regions, this could explain why breeders in southern and other warmer areas have had greater success with breeding for the Onagadori genes.

As an experiment, two test groups were studied over an extended period of time. One group was kept unheated during the winter in a northern climate. The other group was kept at 55°F in the winter.

Repeatedly the unheated group acquired cold-like bronchial symptoms, coughing, and sneezing. The heated group remained unaffected. Does this mean the breed is weak? Not entirely. Could a human being live in the Arctic with only a thin feather coat and no head or leg protection? Hardly. It only means that just as palm trees grow in the warmth of the tropics and Maple trees live in cooler temperate areas, various animals and birds also have their required climates.

Above - A yellow-legged recessive white Onagadori hen.

Other Long Tailed Breeds

While perhaps not having concentrations of Green Jungle Fowl genetics to the degree of the Onagadori, other long tailed breeds do carry some of those same genetics.

The male pictured at the right probably looks much like the ancestors of today's long tailed breeds.

He is a hybrid of a pure Green Jungle Fowl and Ohiki. He contains a sequence of genetics capable of producing a wide variety of color patterns, feather types and body types, as well as carrying the long-crowing gene capable of producing birds which could crow for up to 25 seconds.

Hybrids such as this have probably contributed to the following breeds:

Kurokashiwa

• The Kurokashiwa is a large-fowl breed native to various prefectures in northern Japan. It was developed to have a long, full tail of around two feet in length, but it lacks the ground-dragging saddle that most long tailed breeds exhibit.

The breed features a certain amount of dark pigmentation. The facial skin of hens is black, while that of the males is red spotted with patches of black. The ear lobes of both sexes are red, with or without black pigmentation. This is in contrast to most other long tailed breeds that have white ear lobes.

Above - A Kurokashiwa rooster, King line. Photo courtesy of Marc King

Although it is not usually considered a long-crowing breed, the crow is often as long as that of a Totenko, and is very melodious.

Left - Black Phoenix, Astin line, descendants of the King line of high percentage Kurokashiwa.

Black Phoenix of the King line, possessing a high percentage of Kurokashiwa blood, were imported into the U.S. in 2002 by Toni-Marie Astin and Brian Shamblin. These birds are known to display traits from their Kurokashiwa ancestry, occasionally producing offspring with longer crows and red ear lobes.

Minohiki

• The Minohiki is a large-fowl 'saddle dragging' breed that is native to two prefectures in Japan.

There are two main recognized varieties of the breed. The Mikawa variety is native to the Aichi Prefecture, or the former Mikawa region. The second variety is known as the Enshu variety. It is native to the former Enshu region which is now the Shizuoka Prefecture.

This breed needs similar care to the Phoenix, and can be allowed to walk around naturally, there being no requirement for tomebako. It should be fed a diet low in gluten. Corn-based feed can result in an early death. On such a diet they seldom live past two years of age.

Above - A pair of Minohiki peer into a glass door of the King family home in Italy. Photo courtesy of Marc King.

The King line of Minohiki has been bred to be more resistant to illnesses and corn-based feeds. The latter quality will allow for poultry hobbyists to raise the breed in areas where other feeds are not commonly available.

The abundantly long saddle feathers are achieved through a cycle of molting these feathers only once every two years. Only males showing this trait should be used in breeding. Likewise, only females fathered by individuals with this trait should be used for breeding.

Ohiki

• The Ohiki is said to have been developed in the late Edo period in Kochi, and remains a popular breed in Japan, and among the few European and North American enthusiasts.

It was once considered to be a bantam version of the Minohiki, but its true origins are perhaps lost in history. It is said that in some areas the breed was also called by the name Minohiki. Since it was thought to have descended also in part from the Japanese Chabo, it was then called "Minohiki-Chabo" to distinguish it from the large-fowl Minohiki. It is likely that this name fell out of use when Japanese breeders came to a realization that the breed likely does not descend from the Chabo or the Minohiki. It was more likely to be in the same grouping as other long tailed breeds of the Kochi Prefecture.

Today in Japan, and the other countries to which it has spread, the accepted name for this breed is Ohiki.

Its stature is short due to small legs which are set quite forward on the body, which is somewhat broad, especially at the shoulders.

Its care and rearing is the same as that of other long tailed breeds; not requiring to be kept in tomebako as the Onagadori. It flourishes on a nutritious diet low in corn and other glutenous grains.

Whenever seen, it amuses many by its waddling motion as it strolls casually along the ground with its tail and saddle plumage trailing behind.

Kept dry and on a deep layer of soft bedding, these little fowl stay remarkably clean considering the amount of dragging plumage.

The breed does best in runs. If kept in cages, they should be capable of containing a layer of bedding without it being scratched out by the birds. A cage which has walls with a wooden lower half and a wire upper half will work well. Three feet square and at least eighteen inches in height will provide enough room for a rooster and two hens.

Left - An Ohiki flock of the Astin line. Toni-Marie Astin and Brian Shamblin imported the first Ohiki eggs into the United States in 2002 from Switzerland with the help of Marc King.

Left - These silver duckwing Ohiki were bred by Marc King in Switzerland from the Wolfgang Vits line in Germany. Photo courtesy of Marc King.

As with any long tailed breed, it is best to use covered water dishes to prevent the tail plumage from dragging through the water and becoming soiled. A plastic milk container with a hole cut in the side works well.

Other aspects of the breed's care are similar to those relevant to other breeds of chicken.

Phoenix

• Despite its usual classification as an Asiatic breed, the Phoenix (fē-nĭks) is a European and American breed which was developed in the nineteenth century. They descend only partially from Asian long tailed fowl breeds. Some of the other breeds in their background are Modern Game and Leghorn. Phoenix are hardier birds than Onagadori or fowl containing high percentages of Onagadori blood, and do not require winter heating in most climates.

Left - A Phoenix trio from the Ismer line. The tail is fully grown in this photo. Unlike male Onagadori, male Phoenix molt their tail plumage every one to two years. Photo courtesy of Marc King.

Shokoku

• The Shokoku is a Japanese long tailed breed, duckwing in color (usually silver), with red earlobes and yellow legs. A duckwing Phoenix resembles the breed apart from this earlobe and leg coloration. It molts regularly.

The Shokoku, or an earlier form of the breed, is thought to be the ancestor of most Japanese long tailed breeds. Even though it shows no immediate or direct genetic link to other breeds it could still be an ancient ancestor. It carries a less reliable version of the non-molting gene, but does not readily express the trait.

Above - A Shokoku rooster crows on a gravel path. Photo courtesy of Mitsuyoshi Tatematsu.

Totenko

• This breed has the distinction of being both a long tailed and long crowing breed. Many of the Japanese breeds are indigenous to a particular prefecture. The Totenko however is very widespread throughout Japan and can be found in many areas; also there are enthusiasts keeping the breed in Europe.

Totenko are black breasted red in plumage, with willow / green legs, white earlobes, and single comb.

It molts its two to three foot long tail feathers regularly as do most long tailed breeds. What sets this breed apart is the length of the crow, which can vary from ten to twenty plus seconds. The main priority in breeding Totenko is the crow. Feathering is a secondary consideration in selection and is less easily lost than the crow from generation to generation.

The breed carries hidden genes. From time to time offspring of this clean-legged breed will appear with feathered shanks and vulture hocks. Birds exhibiting these traits do not meet the breed's standard in appearance, but are not culled if the crow is of good quality. Breeding such individuals back into the gene pool perpetuates these hidden traits, which resurface again in future generations. This demonstrates the priority of the crow in the selection of breeding stock.

Though the Totenko is not known to exist in the US at this time, it could be reconstructed using the long tailed and long-crowing genetics already known to exist in various fowl.

Left - Totenko roosters of the Keeling line enjoy the outdoors on a sunny day. Photo courtesy of Julia Keeling.

Housing

Housing for hens, young birds, and breeding flocks -
As discussed under the Breed History and Development, heated winter quarters seem to be essential when keeping Onagadori in temperate and cold climates. A small building or room free of drafts may be insulated well enough to be heated inexpensively even in the middle of winter. The building or room should be predator-proof, and must be kept clean and sanitary to prevent excess humidity and ammonia generated by waste from reaching toxic levels.

Below - Outdoor pens with roofs to keep out the rain work well in warm climates. These pens are at Onagadori South Feather Farm, Georgia, US, and house birds like the bantam Phoenix pictured below.

Heaters with open flames such as LP gas-powered models should be avoided. The dust from the birds is highly combustible. A small electric floor heater, mounted securely at head height, with metal radiant fins will work if cleaned often. Be sure that any heating source is guarded from the birds and that it is plugged into a Ground Fault Circuit Interrupter. Minimum winter temperature is 50 - 55°F.

Pens for Phoenix and other long tailed breeds, excluding Onagadori, may be left unheated. They should however be protected from drafts in areas experiencing cold winters where temperatures may drop below 10°F.

Pens may be any size as long as space is sufficient for the number of birds that it is intended to house. Breeds should be housed according to size. Large-fowl require more space than bantam breeds.

Bantams may be kept with no less than two square feet of floor space per young bird or adult hen. Large-fowl may require three to four square feet of floor space per young bird of either sex or adult hen. Giving more space will help to protect the birds' feathering.

Housing for Males - To prevent the long tail feathers from being stepped on and broken, adult males of either size classification may require as much as twenty-four square feet. This would be the equivalent of a three foot by eight foot pen.

Pens may be enclosed with chicken wire or hardware cloth wire mesh. Pine wood shavings make a good bedding material; a layer of shavings a few inches deep across the pen floor is recommended. Woods like cedar should be avoided, the oils within the shavings and their dust can cause health problems. Florescent full spectrum lighting should be considered for the building, as it does seem to be beneficial. Parrot breeders have used it for years with great success.

Onagadori and Phoenix have remarkable flying capabilities

compared to other chicken breeds. They have controlled flight from three weeks of age. Their large wings and excellent control of the tail allows for quick turns, dives, and steep climbs in the air; they can also fly over quite long distances.

High perches in the pen are a necessity for exercise, and they should be placed as close to the ceiling as possible, yet still allow the birds headroom while perching. There should also be enough room to allow for landings from the perch to the floor. Ideally, a pen should be nearly as long as it is high, with the perch placed midway for ease of landing on either side.

Onagadori will often roost anywhere from seven to twenty or more feet off the ground; usually the higher the better. Avoid using old tree branches for perches as these may contain parasites. Pine 1in x 4in or 2in x 4in boards with sanded edges work well. The four inch wide surface being the up side for perching. These boards should be sound and securely fixed. Every bird in the pen will attempt to pile onto a single perch, so there should be enough high perches so that every bird has space.

Above - This Schubert line Phoenix rooster roosts high in the rafters in his pen.

Above - A photo featuring one of Mrs. Kubota's pure modern Onagadori at the Onagadori Center, Kochi, Japan. Several tomebako can be seen in the background. The Center was started by the late and dearly missed Mr. Kubota who worked hard to produce a line of healthy birds capable of growing tails up to 44 feet in length. Photo courtesy of Julia Keeling.

The Non-Molting Gene

Since male modern Onagadori and birds containing a high percentage of Onagadori genetics are the only long tailed breed kept in tomebako, this section does not apply to any other type of long tailed fowl. Other long tailed breeds are not kept in this manner.

When males from non-molting lines are five to ten months of age, they can begin to be kept in a tomebako. The best male should be chosen by considering health, temperament, and tail feathering. Those exhibiting a calm temperament with lots of multiple feathering and good length of feathers are the ones to choose to develop further in tomebako. At this time any broken or damaged tail or saddle feathers may be carefully plucked and allowed to re-grow. The tomebako is a wooden box approximately six feet high, three feet wide, and nine inches deep. Its interior construction is such that the bird, the bird's tail, and the droppings tray each has its own compartment. Roosters raised in this manner must have daily contact with their care-givers. At least one hour of exercise and walks is required daily. The males must also be kept warm during the winter, a temperature of at least 50°F to 55°F.

The goal with raising a male in a tomebako is to prevent him from molting or damaging the saddle, sickle, and covert feathers of the tail for an extended period of time, often as long as five years. During this time these feathers should remain in blood-feather and growing at a rate of three feet or more per year. The saddle feathers grow somewhat slower, but should end up at least one third the length of the coverts.

Some people have implied that tomebako are in some way inhumane. This could not be further from the truth. Accurate claims or criticisms regarding this way of rearing cannot be made unless a personal study has been made of the method and the birds involved. The roosters are let out often every day for exercise and handling. They view the tomebako as their territory and will many times fly back to it on their own if their handler lets their guard down while holding and protecting the bird's tail.

The breed's best-known feature, the male's extraordinary tail plumage, is governed by three genetic traits. These have not been officially documented or found in DNA strands. They are simply recorded this way following breeders' observations.

The first and most noticeable trait is the co-dominant quick growth gene, Gt, which is noticeable even when the bird is on the ground, as it causes the feathers to be much longer than other breeds even at a young age.

The second gene causes more than the normal amount of feathers to grow in the tail and saddle region. This dominant trait is referred to as multiple feathering, or simply Mf.

The third gene is the recessive non-molting gene, referred to as nm or mt. Phoenix and other long tailed breeds lack this gene.

Onagadori are Gt/Gt mt/mt Mf/Mf. The slashes and pairing denote homozygosity. Other long tailed breeds, such as Phoenix are Gt/Gt Mt+/Mt+ Mf/Mf, meaning that they have the dominant trait for the regular molting cycle instead of the recessive non-molting trait. Chickens that are not long tailed varieties are gt+/gt+ Mt+/Mt+, meaning that they lack the quick growth trait of the tail and saddle feathers as well as the non-molting trait.

This is the most distinct thing that separates Onagadori from Phoenix. Expression of the mt trait is partially dependent upon environment. Even birds that would express non-molting when raised in a tomebako, may still molt once every one to two years if left to run on the ground. It is only by using tomebako that the hormones controlling the molting cycle are partially suppressed to allow the non-molting trait to be expressed.

Given the recessive nature of the non-molting trait, it is important to realize that not 100% of homozygous birds will express non-molting. Nevertheless, if two individuals carrying this recessive trait are bred together some of their offspring will express the non-molting if raised in tomebako, due to the inheritance of the recessive trait from both parents.

The genetic profile of each feather group: the saddles, coverts, and sickles, must each contain a copy of all three traits: Gt, Mf, and nm (or mt). The main tail feathers should contain Gt and Mf. The main tail feathers molt normally once every twelve to twenty four months. No other breed of fowl has the same combination of these traits as does the Onagadori. It is only when they are combined in this precise manner to ultimate expression, that a bird is clearly an Onagadori.

Four tomebako are the minimum needed in order to achieve the selection for these genetic traits. See Appendix 1 for tomebako building plans.

Dietary Requirements

With the flight of long tailed breeds being so good, it should come as no surprise that they often fly to greet their keeper as soon as they step into the pen, especially if there is food involved, or the birds think there may be. Individual birds will have their own temperaments and some may be more friendly than others: some may choose to land at your feet versus on your shoulder or head. They have two motives for boldness, either they want attention or they want food. Attention is fairly self-explanatory, but the type of foods suitable for these breeds needs specifying.

A good diet will consist of a very natural menu, similar to the wild grains that Jungle Fowl would eat. Grains that are high in gluten like corn, wheat, barley, millet, and milo should be avoided. These grains sometimes pass through the body undigested and the birds then eat them again. In fact such grains would have to pass through a hen's digestion twice for full absorption of all the nutrients. Grains such as oats and brown rice are preferable as they are more digestible. Nutrition is important with all poultry, but especially so with long tailed breeds. Empty foods should be avoided, foods low in nutrition and high in sugars are not good for them.

Protein is a major part of the diet, but the source of that protein must be examined. All proteins are not equal, plant protein is not easily utilized. Neither plant protein nor protein from fowl by-products, such as ground up feathers and bones, will fully meet their nutritional needs. What they need is animal protein, ideally from marine fish. Such fish not only has a type of protein that can be utilized efficiently, but it also has valuable vitamins, omega oils, and essential fatty acids for good health. Many of the birds in Kochi, Japan are fed fish since Kochi is a coastal prefecture and fish is widely available.

However, just as man cannot live on bread alone, Onagadori and other long tailed fowl cannot live on fish and grain alone. Fish should only be used for the portion of the diet that would usually be filled by insects, worms, and other prey if the birds were foraging. Oats and brown rice can be used for the bulk of the diet, or if those are not readily available, a good quality lamb and rice dog food can be substituted.

Dark green leafy vegetables such as romaine lettuce, spinach, or dandelion greens are also useful foods for the flock.

Fruits such as cranberries, containing antioxidants and having other beneficial properties, are also recommended.

Vitamins, minerals, and calcium in particular should be added to the food. Local feed mills can advise you on what products they have and how much to add. Each pre-mixed additive is different, but, if available, real vitamins should always be chosen over synthetic ones. The best source for minerals is kelp meal, which should be added into the feed at a rate of 1% to 2 %.

Oyster shell calcium will help with the bone formation in young birds and with shell formation in laying hens so that the egg production does not deplete the calcium in their bones.

Every breeder has a mix that works best for them. Onagadori breeder Mrs. Kubota once stated, "Whatever you eat, your birds can eat. And whatever your birds can eat, you can eat." It should be kept in mind that she was not speaking about foods of a western culture. Asian diets are focused around rice, fish, vegetables, and fruits; these are what she was suggesting were a healthy diet for long tailed fowl. So it was not being stated that pizza and burgers were acceptable foods for the fowl.

The goal is to produce a diet that works for the birds, is balanced, and is around 18% to 22% protein. Feathers are 90% protein. The protein amount is important to an extent, but even more important is the quality of that protein. Below is a list of the approximate protein percentages of various foods.

Food	Protein %	Feeding Information
Brown Rice	7%	Feed cooked only.
Cranberries	0%	Feed only a few each day. Too many cranberries can cause the birds to pass large amounts of water.

Protein percentages of various foods continued -

Food	Protein %	Feeding information
Fish meal	60%	5 lbs. per 100 lbs. of other feed as a grower ration for young birds, or a flock maintenance ration for mature birds. Eight pounds per 100 lbs. of other feed as a breeder ration.
Fish, raw	28%	Raw fish has many nutrients, but should be only a small part of the diet.
Hard Boiled Egg (whole with shell)	49%	Egg whites are a complete protein and the body absorbs 96% of the egg's protein. It makes total sense that eggs would be a great treat food for birds. Boil for 15 minutes to kill any pathogens and bacteria that may be in the egg. Let cool before offering it to the bird. Eggs should be only a small part of the diet.
Kelp Meal	5%	Only add 1 to 2 lbs. per 100 lbs. of other feed. Kelp contains salt. Adding it at a rate of more than 2% can cause there to be dangerous levels of salt in the feed.
Whole oats	14%	Whole oats is one of the few grains from which the birds can digest and utilize the nutrients.

Below - An example of a corn-free ration.

Whole oats	75 lbs.
Bean Meal	7.5 lbs.
Vitamin and nutrients mix	7.5 lbs. (figured as 44% protein in this case)
Fish Meal	5 lbs. per 100 lbs. of other feed as a grower ration for young birds or flock maintenance ration for mature birds. Eight pounds per 100 lbs. of other feed as a breeder ration.
Soy oil	3 lbs. Soy products contain phytoestrogens. An excess of soy can adversely affect the hens' productive life. Alfalfa can have the same affect.
Calcium	2.5 lbs.
Kelp	2 lbs.
Vitamins A, D, and E	1.25 lbs.

The grower ration is approximately 17% protein. The breeder ration is approximately 18% protein.

This food analysis was conducted by an avian veterinarian. It was found to be a balanced diet for domestic chickens requiring high amounts of protein.

Once a diet has been established, it is good practice to allow Onagadori, and birds of predominantly Onagadori genetics, to fast once a week after five months of age, giving only water on this day.

On the day preceding and the day following the fasting day, the birds should be fed only a mix of cooked brown rice, cooked rolled oats, raw (or lightly cooked) fish, fruit, vegetables, and hard-boiled egg. The shells should be included and everything crumbled together in a food processor. This mix is mostly liquids and helps to cleanse the bird's digestive system of toxins produced from digesting grains.

Fasting is not necessary for long tailed breeds other than Onagadori, the usual ration may be given every day of the week. Fresh fruits and vegetables may occasionally be given as a supplement, but should be given in moderation to avoid diluting the nutrition of the main ration.

Above - A breeding pen with an Astin line Phoenix rooster and hens of mixed long tailed breed backgrounds. Some of the birds' feathers are broken. This regularly happens in a breeding pen.

Breeding

Breeding techniques are a major topic of discussion with these fowl. Choosing a pairing should be based upon various considerations, all of which will influence the following generation. Not only must due thought be given to the choice of the two individuals involved, but the qualities of each bird's father must also be examined.

A pairing should first be based upon health. If both birds are healthy, the next consideration is their relationship to each other. If they are siblings, mating should be avoided. Line-breeding father to daughter, son to mother, nephew to aunt, uncle to niece, and grandchildren to grandparents is acceptable, but mating siblings is not advisable. This would combine the same recessive genetic traits as line breeding, but with the disadvantage of possibly producing birds which are homozygous for bad or weak genes.

However, breeding siblings together for only one generation will usually reveal most recessive traits. The resulting offspring can be useful birds with which to breed, as good and bad traits can surface, revealing what needs to be bred out and what traits need perpetuating. If these inbred birds are used, it should be to out-cross birds of good type and resistance.

The lineage of every bird in a flock should be known by the breeder. A flock size of forty hens and ten roosters is a suitable basis for starting a serious breeding program. This obviously takes some time to achieve as only the best birds are selected from those raised.

If an out-cross to another line or breed is made, it must be done for a purpose and with a definite plan to get back to pure. The first few generations will carry recessive traits from the other parent. Heterozygous stock should never be considered as being the pure breed. The offspring should be bred back to a pure individual for a several generations. By F4, with good selection, the birds should be homozygous.

The purity percentage of a given generation is calculated by adding together the purity percentages of the two parents and dividing by two. For example: the first generation of an out-cross (F1) would be 100 + 0 = 100. 100 divided by 2 = 50%. So the resulting offspring would be 50% purebred. The F2 generation, from F1 bred to pure would be 50 + 100 = 150. Divide 150 by 2, and it can be seen that F2s would be 75% pure. The same formula applies to F3, F4, and so on.

Feathering should of course be a major consideration. Has the male expressed all of the desired traits? Has the female's father done the same? If not, is it suspected that each line carries the required recessive traits to make up for these shortcomings? Both parents should have ample multiple feathering. If the father is short in this, the female can pass on the trait to the offspring. In fact it transmits more easily from the female to the offspring than from the male.

Another very important aspect of choosing parents for the next generation is looking at the body types of each parent. Are they sturdy? Do they have any skeletal weaknesses? If the answer to any of these questions is yes, either another parent should be chosen, or the breeder should be positive that the other parent more than compensates for any weaknesses that parent may possess.

Breeders of other fowl often speculate about how fertilization is accomplished without the male's cumbersome tail being an obstruction. Only the best males are used for breeding. Once Onagadori have gone at least four years without molting the saddle, sickle, and covert feathers, they are removed from the tomebako. At this time, the long feathers are cut back to only two feet or less in length. The male can then be placed into a breeding pen with hens. Strong healthy males may fertilize four to six hens.

Diet plays a crucial role in breeding these birds. To help increase fertility they should be switched to a higher protein feed approximately one month prior to breeding. Once the male is placed with hens, breeding may not occur for several days or even for a week or more. Males that have been raised in tomebako are bonded more closely to their handler than other birds and also have low hormone levels. They will not start being reproductive until they go through courtship with the hens, their hormones increase, and they figure out what to do.

If the breeder is reluctant to cut off the male's extravagant feather growth for breeding, they may consider holding the male's tail up and out of the way for a few minutes instead. They would probably have to do this several times before he does mate due to the factors discussed above. Even so, the fluctuation of hormones can cause the male's tail feathers to dry up and come out of blood-feather, thus causing them to be molted anyway.

A male that has molted many feathers at once may be sore for some time. He needs to be handled with care; the skin around the new pin-feathers will be tender.

There is also another breeding method that can be considered, this being artificial insemination. While this puts less stress on the male, to him it is still a form of breeding and can result in escalated hormone levels. However it is achieved, breeding can potentially cause the male to molt his saddle, sickle, and covert feathers.

Once breeding has ceased and the previously non-molting male is placed back into a tomebako, the feather groups expressing the non-molting trait will once again begin to grow without molting for an extended period, hopefully several years.

Phoenix, and other long tailed breeds that molt normally, are not affected in this way and do not require such specialized treatment.

With such a high level of animal husbandry, Onagadori and Phoenix tend to have a much longer life span than other poultry breeds. It can range from eight to twelve years, although their fertility seldom last beyond four to six years. However, breeders rarely dispose of prized males after they lose fertility, but allow them to continue growing their tails, and see what can be expected from their offspring.

The most common colors are fairly standard. Colors can be mixed, but in some cases, it may take a few generations to clean back up to a standard color.

See page 30 for a list of some usual results, but there are many exceptions not listed.

Color of Parents	Color of Offspring
Same colors bred together	Same color as parents.
Same colors bred together, but each carrying recessive white	50% of the offspring will be same color as parents and the other 50% will be white.
Black-breasted red (BBR) x gold	Mostly bbr, but with some dark gold offspring.
BBR x silver	Dirty silver to blonde, medium gold, with an occasional bbr offspring of the opposite sex to the bbr parent.
Gold x silver	This combination is usually sex-linked, with offspring being the same color as the opposite sex parent. Silver will usually be slightly dirty and gold lighter than the gold parent.
White x any duckwing color	Being a recessive color, the white bird is actually not genetically white. Silver duckwing is the most common color for white birds to be carrying, but any color is possible. If the white bird is genetically silver, use the silver combinations above to estimate the outcome.

A chart like the one below is useful for keeping breeding records.

Cock	Hen	Date Bred	# Of Eggs Laid & Batch #	Date Set	Date Hatched

Left - Yellow-legged recessive white chicks of high Onagadori percentage (Rogers line) at two weeks of age. These birds are carrying silver duckwing coloration, hence the single black dot on the head. This dot will be lost at the birds' first molt.

The internal structure of an egg is pictured below left. It is vital for chick development that an egg should not be shaken or turned small end up. This can disturb the arrangement of the various internal layers within the egg and ruin its viability for hatching.

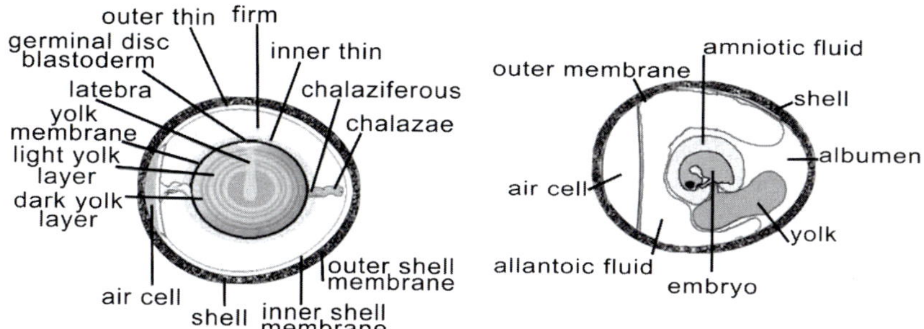

Above left - An egg prior to incubation.
Above right - Embryo at approximately 10 days of development.

During development, shown above right, the chick's head is at the large end near the air cell. When candling an egg, the air cell should be stationary and not be seen moving around as the egg is gently turned around horizontally.

Three further membranes form within the developing fertilized egg. These are the amnion, chorion, and allantois membranes, not shown in the illustration. The amnion is a fluid-filled sac within which the embryo develops. The allantois membrane is an extension of the embryo's digestive tract; it fuses with the chorion to form the chorioallantoic membrane. This membrane contains the many blood vessels that collect oxygen through the shell, carrying it to the developing embryo, and take carbon dioxide back out of the egg during incubation.

At the time of hatching, the blood supply recedes from these vessels and they then dry up. The resulting dried tissue falls off shortly after hatching.

Once fertile eggs are being produced, an increase in flock numbers can begin. Fertile eggs may be kept for up to two weeks at 55ºF, or for less time at a slightly higher temperature. It is important not to wash any eggs that are to be incubated, as the microscopic sediment in water will plug the tiny pores in the shell and prevent oxygen from getting to the embryo. The eggs should be stored in cardboard egg cartons turned up on their sides, and the eggs or entire carton should be turned from side to side daily. Eggs should never be turned small-end-up as it can destroy the air cell on which the embryo depends during incubation. This would render the egg incapable of producing a chick.

After several eggs have been collected, incubation can begin. There are two basic ways to incubate eggs, either by broody hens or by incubator. Hens of long tailed breeds often go broody and make good mothers, and hatch rates are many times better with this method than with an incubator.

Sometimes several hens in one pen may lay and go broody at the same time. If this happens they may form a communal nest, laying their eggs collectively and jointly brood the eggs and hatch the young. However this can occasionally cause the problem of eggs being accidentally broken. Depending upon the temperament of the hens, one may choose to raise all of the chicks herself after hatching and chase the other hens away.

Usually all of the hens may still share the responsibility of motherhood, serving as a communal nursery for the young.

Above - A nest box

If there are no broody hens available of the same breed when there are enough eggs saved, it is perfectly acceptable to use another breed of hen as a foster mother. Bantam Cochin and Silkie crosses often work well.

A hen can be made to go broody by placing her in a medium sized individual cage or pen with a nest box, in a quiet, dimly lit, and less busy part of the building. Feed and water should be located near by. A nest box like the one above will provide some privacy for a setting hen. It should be of sufficient size and have a perch on the front for easier access.

If she is given golf balls, ping-pong balls, or dummy eggs this will help encourage her to go broody. Once she is setting on her artificial clutch of eggs, they should be replaced by the real eggs, at night and with the lights out. Be sure that the hen gets off of the nest regularly to feed, drink, and defecate.

Once the broody hen has hatched the brood around 21 to 23 days later, she must now have a cage large enough for her and the chicks to have plenty of room. The chicks must be able to reach the water source and the container must be of a design that will not pose any threat of drowning. Some chick starter crumbles should be available in a small dish for them. The hen will eat it this as well as her regular food during this time, which is fine.

After she has raised the young for a couple of months, she may be placed back with her flock. This is best done at night, but care must be taken to observe, at first light in the morning, that the flock accepts her back. The pecking order will have changed in her absence, and they may be more aggressive towards her or may not accept her at all, although that would be very unusual. Onagadori in particular are very rarely aggressive. However, as with any other breed, pecking order displays can go too far. Most other long tailed breeds tend to be slightly more territorial than Onagadori, so they may not as easily accept back a flock member after its absence. If too much aggression is shown, a flock must be found that will accept her, or she must be placed in a new pen of her own. The offspring may be placed in a larger pen of their own.

Incubators work quite well as long as they are accurate, but most breeders have a particular kind of incubator that they prefer. They come in various sizes and with various features; the type to select depends upon your requirements.

There are two basic kinds of incubator: still-air and forced-air. Still-air incubators rely solely on passive air exchange to supply the eggs with fresh air. Forced-air models have a small fan that keeps all the eggs heated more evenly.

Small incubators usually hold around four dozen medium sized eggs. Larger incubators can hold hundreds of eggs.

There are also different types of thermostat: manual and digital. Manual thermostats may often need adjusting since the incubator's temperature can fluctuate with the surrounding air temperature. Digital thermostats are factory preset to the 99.5ºF range. This keeps the incubator at an even temperature even if the surrounding air temperature fluctuates a few degrees.

Most breeders also have a preferred method of incubation, but this is the most common method:

Eggs should be saved over a couple of weeks and stored at 55-65ºF, until there is a suitable number for the incubator. The eggs should be left to warm at room temperature prior to placing them in the incubator. Letting the eggs warm will prevent them from sweating as they would if placed directly into the incubator from cool storage. As already mentioned, liquids on the outside of the egg can plug the pores in the shell.

Some sources claim that 101ºF is best for chicken eggs. Most long tailed breeds do better if incubated slightly cooler at 99.5°F to 100°F. The use of an accurate thermometer is essential. Small amounts of water should be added to the incubator for humidity, as directed by the manufacturer. Better yet is the valuable advice of a well-experienced poultry breeder.

After placing the eggs into the incubator it should not be opened or the eggs turned for thirty-six hours. From then until the eighteenth day the eggs should be turned three times daily. Some incubators have automatic turning trays. This additional mechanism decreases the number of eggs that can fit into the incubator, and as with anything, turners can fail. Therefore, if an automatic turner is chosen over manual turning of the eggs, it should be checked daily to ensure that it is working properly.

The incubator should not be opened after the eighteenth day unless there is an absolute necessity - having to add water or something else of importance. Every time the incubator is opened, valuable humidity is lost.

Around day five to seven the eggs can be candled. A specially made device available from poultry retailers can be used; or a piece of cardboard with a small round hole in it nearly the size of the egg, placed over a strong flashlight, is equally effective. With either method a strong light is shone through the egg to reveal the inner contents. If developing, an embryo will look somewhat like a small kidney bean with a spider web surrounding it. The webbing is the blood vessels that attach the embryo to its nutrient source, the yolk sac, and to the inner membrane of the egg. Eggs that do not show any development after one week are infertile and can be removed from the incubator.

Bad eggs left in the incubator for longer periods of time may explode. Once experienced, this will never be forgotten.

The chicks will hatch on or around the twenty-first day. It will usually take around twenty-four hours for a chick to hatch after it makes the first small hole in the shell. This hole is referred to as a pip. The pip should appear on the top side of the egg at the large end.

The chicks will begin to walk a couple of hours after hatching, but should be left in the incubator for 12 to 24 hours. During this time the down feathers will dry, fluff out and become insulating. A newly hatched chick will not need food or water for 24 hours after hatching, as it will still be receiving nutrients from the yolk sac that has now been absorbed into the abdomen.

When the chicks are removed from the incubator, they should be placed in a preheated brooder, or cardboard box with a heat lamp. Brooder temperature should be, on average, between 95ºF and 97ºF. If the chicks are too cold they will huddle under the heat source. If too hot, they will get as far away from the heat source as they can, and perhaps pant and / or hold their wings away from their bodies. When they freely roam around their new home, it will be apparent that the heat is just right. The temperature of the brooder can be dropped 5º a week until a temperature of 70ºF is reached, but this should only be done if the chicks appear to still be warm with each 5º decrease in temperature.

Small plastic can lids may be used as water and feed containers for the first few days. Clean peanut butter can lids work well. Once the chicks are a week old the lids can be replaced with regular chick feeders and drinkers that are available from local farm stores.

The chicks should be fed with starter crumble until they are a month old. After that time, they should be slowly weaned onto the breeders' regular ration mix. This should be done by mixing the two feeds together, so that over the period of a week the regular ration is added to the starter in increasing proportions, until they are on the new ration only.

When the chicks begin eating whole grains, grit, usually obtainable in the form of ground oyster shell, should be provided to aid digestion. Small amounts should be sprinkled on top of their food. Such grit will also give the birds beneficial calcium. The birds store the grit in their gizzards, and as the gizzard muscle works to digest the food, the grit grinds grains and other foods into a finer substance to be further digested. The nutrients can then be absorbed into the body.

Below - A batch chart like this one will make it easier to record details of offspring.

Batch # & Notes	# Of Chicks In Batch	Band # & Color	Sex
______	______	______	______
		______	______
Notes		______	______
		______	______
		______	______
		______	______
		______	______
		______	______

Left - A young silver duckwing adolescent female of high Onagadori percentage, Rogers line, enjoying the shade of a willow tree.

Caring for Adolescent Birds

Young five to eight month old birds are already on an adult feed ration, but at five months of age, youngsters of high Onagadori percentage go under another dietary change. They now have enough body mass to begin fasting one day a week. On the day before and the day after fasting they should be fed a mix that is mostly liquid. It should consist of equal parts cooked brown rice and rolled oats, with some hard-boiled eggs, raw (or lightly broiled) fish, fruit, and vegetables mixed with it. All of the ingredients are then crumbled together in a food processor. This mix helps to clean out the bird's digestive system. This is the permanent regime that such birds should remain on throughout their lives. The fast should only be suspended in the event that a bird becomes unwell.

Adolescent birds still have need of more warmth than adults. Between 60ºF and 70ºF would be the minimum temperature. They should also be kept out of any drafts.

They may be kept in large numbers in large pens, or in smaller numbers in smaller pens or cages. The space allotment of three square feet of floor space per bird can be used as a general guide. Several cockerels may be kept in one pen of sufficient size, Onagadori are usually not aggressive, although from time to time there may be an exception. Pens should be monitored closely as attitudes and pecking order can change quickly in adolescent birds. If a temperament problem with any individual develops within the pen, that bird should be removed to another pen or cage. This is not a frequent problem, but it can happen.

Onagadori are not typically feather pickers, but if they are cramped for space or short on protein in their diet it may become a habit. Phoenix and other long tailed breeds are more prone to this habit, but it depends heavily upon the temperament of individual birds. There are three remedies for this problem. One being that the hook on the end of the upper mandible can be trimmed, with guillotine type dog nail clippers, to just below the blood vessel running almost to the tip. This will re-grow quickly and require repeated trimming. If the blood vessel is accidentally severed, the bleeding can be stopped with cayenne powder or blood stop powder, or the cut can be cauterized with a soldering iron, being careful not to burn the inside of the mouth.

If picking becomes a problem, only remove the very end of the hook of the upper mandible to just past the end of the lower mandible.

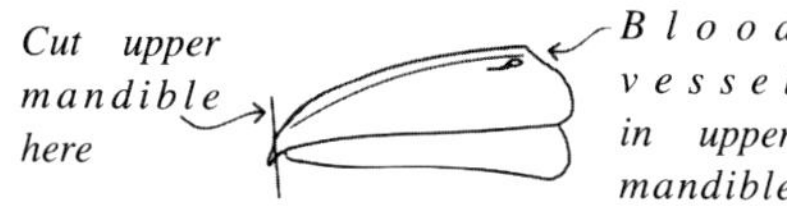

The second option would be to remove the guilty individual to a solitary pen or cage. The offending bird will usually be easy to identify, being the one with the most feathers.

Third, it could be removed from the breeding program and allowed to run loose outdoors. If in a warm climate, it will do well running loose if given some protection from predators. Picking will usually subside once the bird is given free run of larger spaces.

Breeding with such a bird is not recommended unless there is no other option. The undesirable behavior is partially a hereditary tendency and partially a learned behavior. It can be culled out of a flock if it appears, so is rare in quality stock.

One behavioral problem more likely to appear in a flock is egg eating. This can happen if a hen is lacking in some nutrition or if she just learns, usually through an egg getting broken somehow, that raw eggs are something she likes. Beak trimming is not likely to help with this problem, a hen will still find a way to break the eggs. Dummy eggs teach the birds that they cannot break eggs. The artificial eggs can be made of nearly anything non-toxic and sturdy - wood, ceramic, even cement, and can be included in any nest. If painted, a non-toxic paint should be used.

Culling, Selecting for Quality

Flock improvement is achieved by selective breeding and culling, by only breeding with the best of the best. Keeping stock with too many faults would be contrary to breeding goals.

Culling for health should be the breeder's number one priority. If bred with and relied upon for producing future generations of stock, one bird of low resistance can create an entire line of failing birds. Sick birds that do not recover after proper treatment should not leave your property.

A question often asked is how to cull humanely without inflicting pain to the ill bird. One method is to quickly sever the neck, well below the base of the head, with an axe over a chopping block. This is most effective and painless if done swiftly.

Culling is not pleasant, nor is it easy to do. Whatever culling method is chosen for an ill bird, it is done to protect the flock and breeding program.

Another reason to cull is when there are faults in type and feathering. Personal goals for the flock's appearance, or a written standard of perfection, should be used to choose which birds to cull or not use for breeding. Healthy birds need not be culled, but may be given away to others as pets, yard birds, or layers, but birds with faults should never be given or sold to anyone planning to breed them. This would only hurt the breed as well as the donor's reputation.

Birds with obvious defects such as health problems or crooked beaks may be culled early. However, when culling is considered because of feather or color traits it must be remembered that feathering can change as the bird matures. A long tailed fowl should never be culled due to its feathering prior to its first molt and the acquisition of adult plumage. It must also be born in mind that health, feather quality, and type should always take priority over coloration.

A well-written and detailed plan will help a breeder decide on the path to take in order to improve their poultry and reach their goal.

On the following pages is a standard to help a breeder decide what to aim for when selecting for the non-molting trait. Birds that do not exhibit these traits may be considered for culling.

It can be repeated that health is the first priority, followed by feathering; both of these ahead of all other considerations.

Co-Author David Rogers' Onagadori Standard

Shape of Male -

Comb: Single, medium in size, red in color, 5 even points, set firmly upon the head without folding over, blade should be small and neat without projecting down the back of the head.

Beak: Moderate in length, strong, curving moderately

Face: Full, smooth, free of wrinkles, and medium to light red in color

Eyes: Round and red-brown in color

Wattles: Medium, well rounded at lower edges, free from wrinkles and folds

Ear Lobes: Large, white in color, elongated oval, smooth, free from wrinkles or folds

Head: Unexaggerated, moderate in length and depth

Neck: Moderately long, carried upright

Hackle: Abundant, soft and fine textured, falling gracefully over and past the shoulders

Back: Moderate in length and breadth, straight, rounding at the shoulders, sloping downward slightly towards the tail

Wings: Large in size, held close to the body near horizontal drooping only slightly, held slightly below the rump. Bows - smooth, well rounded. Covers - broad feathers. Primaries - broad, convex and tapering towards the rear, completely hidden by secondaries. Secondaries - moderate in breadth and strong

Breast: Full and soft feathered

Body & Stern: Moderate in length and depth

Legs & Toes: Legs - Set well apart when viewed from the front, placed midway on body when viewed from the side. Strong and medium in length. Toes- Long, straight, four on each foot, and evenly spread. Color - yellow in white birds, willow in all other colored birds.

Lower Thighs: Moderate in length

Shanks: Moderate in length

Spurs: Strong and hard, and set low on the leg

Coverts: Twelve feet or more long, growing at least 32 inches per year, the more the better. Not molting for at least four years, ideally five, not counting first molt losing juvenile feathering. Top Coverts - Multiple, thin, soft in texture, following the contour of part of the tail then limp and falling downward. Under-tail Coverts (Crissum) - Multiple, six inches in length or longer, medium in width, soft in texture, slightly rounded at the ends.

Tail: Somewhat wide and near flat width ways, but not excessively spread. Multiple feathering i.e. more than six feathers on each side. Main tail - thin feathers but wider than coverts, soft, moderately limp, and full. Sloping downward from the back and well below horizontal. 1/4 to 1/3 the length of the coverts.

Main Sickles and Lesser (Mutant) Sickles: Fine and soft textured. Lesser (Mutant) sickles not molting for at least four years, ideally five after first molt to lose juvenile feathering.

Saddles: Covering the ends of the wings, at least 1/3 to 1/2 the length of the coverts, not molting for four years, ideally five, not counting first molt losing juvenile feathering.

Shape of Female -

Comb: Single, medium in size, red in color, five even points, set firmly upon the head without folding over, blade should be small and neat without projecting down the back of the head.

Beak: Moderate in length, strong, curving moderately

Face: Full, smooth, free of wrinkles, and medium to light red in color

Eyes: Round and red-brown in color

Wattles: Small, well rounded at lower edges, free from wrinkles and folds

Ear Lobes: Moderately sized, white in color, elongated oval, smooth, free from wrinkles or folds, and firm textured

Head: Unexaggerated, moderate in length and depth

Neck: Moderately long, well arched

Hackle: Abundant, soft and fine textured, falling gracefully over the shoulders, joining closely in the front of the neck

Back: Moderate in length and breadth, straight, rounding at the shoulders, sloping downward slightly towards the tail.

Wings: Large in size, held close to the body near horizontal, held slightly below the rump. Bows - smooth, well rounded. Covers - broad feathers. Primaries - broad, convex and tapering towards the rear, completely hidden by secondaries. Secondaries - moderate in breadth and strong

Breast: Full and soft feathered

Body & Stern: Moderate in length and depth

Legs & Toes: Legs - Set well apart when viewed from the front, placed midway on body when viewed from the side. Strong and medium in length. Toes - Long, straight, four on each foot, and evenly spread. Color - yellow in white birds, willow in all other colored birds.

Lower Thighs: Moderate in length

Shanks: Moderate in length

Spurs: Usually present. Should be strong, but not overly large.

Coverts: Top Coverts - Multiple, moderately thin, soft in texture, following the contour of the tail. Lower Coverts - Multiple, thin, soft in texture, rounded at the ends

Tail: Somewhat wide and near flat width ways, but not excessively spread. Multiple feathering i.e. more than six feathers on each side, moderately long, slightly convex to near flat in shape, molting normally unlike the male. Main tail - thin feathers, soft, and full. Sloping downward from the back and well below horizontal.

APPEARANCE: The most prominent characteristic of the breed is the multiple feathering in the tails of both sexes and the non-molting of the male's tail. The body of both sexes should have a game or Jungle Fowl type build with body held high and well balanced on legs of moderate length. The hens should also have long tails such that the coverts extend beyond the main tail feathers. The male's tail should be extreme and excessive in length, twelve feet or longer. Special attention and care must be given the male's tail in order that it remains in good, clean, unbroken condition. Standard weights: cock 64 oz., hen 48 oz.

The standard for Phoenix, and long tailed breeds other than Onagadori, may be viewed in a variety of poultry publications.

Socialization

Onagadori and most Phoenix are very people oriented, in fact many prefer human company to that of their own kind. This human contact helps to reduce stress in the daily life of the flock. The birds depend on their keeper for this socialization as well as for the necessities such as food and housing. Just being held for a few minutes at a time seems to soothe them and give them pleasure. Even though they are quieter than most other chickens, they are vocal creatures and communicate by voice as well as by body language, largely following the mainly dawn and dusk Jungle Fowl vocalization pattern. It is very apparent that they have the ability to recognize and distinguish voices, and they will certainly recognize their keeper's voice and seem to enjoy being talked to.

The concept of chickens requiring and actually preferring human contact in this way is not often considered or discussed. Many breeds only become tame when their handlers start to devote more contact time to them, but Onagadori seem to hatch tame and stay that way. It is almost as if they crave contact with their handler, pacing the edge of the pen closest to them until they are given some attention. Long, low, broken note coaxing vocalizations may accompany the behavior, and this is not displayed just when the food dish is empty, it usually happens whenever the keeper approaches.

Males from non-molting lines, kept in tomebako, are even

friendlier than birds kept in pens. They prefer the security of their tomebako to being in the open, and the constant company of their keeper while they are on the ground for exercise, is beneficial. To the bird being reared in a tomebako, their keeper is their flock and as such, they provide security and "conversation." Males will easily bond with their handler and even offer bits of food to their human companion. If down at their level, it is not uncommon for them to hop up into their handler's lap to sun bathe, start a conversation, or to be stroked on their back or under the wings.

Left - Handling birds often will also make them easier to exhibit. This Astin line Phoenix rooster was shown by Josiah Jones and placed well in the show.

Right - Handling birds often will also familiarize the bird with physical exams such as checking the status of blood feathers as shown here with an Onagadori rooster. Photo courtesy of Marc King.

Above - Two male modern Onagadori. This line is the work of the late Mr. Tajima. Onagadori are often taken out of doors for photographing. A well kept garden is a fine backdrop for these amazing fowl. A tarp has been laid out on the wet ground here to protect the tail plumage. Photo courtesy of Julia Keeling.

Grooming

Daily contact with Onagadori, or birds being raised in that manner, will allow the birds to become accustomed to regular maintenance. This includes the trimming of toe nails, spurs, and the upper mandible, all of which have an accelerated growth rate on Onagadori. Phoenix have a similar accelerated growth rate in these areas, although not as rapid as Onagadori, and trimming should be practiced as needed.

As discussed in a previous chapter, the upper mandible may need to be trimmed with the guillotine type of dog nail clippers if feather picking becomes a problem. While this is rare in quality stock, the upper mandible may still require trimming if it grows too long and impairs eating. In this case the lower tip of the upper mandible should be trimmed so that it just slightly over-hangs the tip of the lower mandible.

The lower mandible seldom needs trimming. There is very little margin for error due to the layout of the interior of the mouth, the flesh within it, and the blood vessel being in such close proximity to the tip. If this should ever need to be trimmed, a nail file is preferable to clippers, work being done carefully, shaping according to the proper profile.

Toe nails may also be trimmed with the same clippers, care being taken not to cut through the blood vessel running most of the length of the nail. If needed, backlighting the nail with a strong light will help locate this vein. Caution must be used in order not to burn the bird's foot if the light is particularly hot. Anything close to, or above, the bird's body temperature of nearly 105ºF is too hot to hold near a bird's flesh. With birds of lighter pigmentation, such as whites and silvers, it is relatively easy to locate the blood vessels in the nails; those of birds with darker pigmentation, such as black-breasted reds and golds, may be more difficult to see. If a nail vein is severed, blood-stop powder, cayenne pepper powder, or a heated soldering iron will stop the bleeding. An antibiotic ointment on any open cut, or recently scabbed area, may be beneficial in preventing infections.

As with the mandibles and toe nails, the spurs also have an inner blood supply. Spurs grow continuously and will need to be trimmed for two major reasons: First, a male may unintentionally hurt a female with his spurs while mating; second, the spurs may grow to such a length as to impair walking or setting. Spur trimming is more difficult than nail trimming. It is sometimes suggested that a mechanical rotary tool with a cutting disk can be used to cut the spurs to within one inch from the leg. This is not a safe means of trimming spurs, as friction from the quickly moving cutting surface heats up the spur and causes the bird to experience a severe hot flash. This can stress a bird to the point of death.

The best way to trim a bird's spur is for the leg to be firmly held, close to the spur. Then, with a pair of pliers, the spur should be gripped close to the leg, and twisted counter-clockwise. The spur naturally grows as a series of cones, and the outer portion of this stack of cones will twist free from the inner cones. This shortens the spur by around half of an inch. After twisting the outer portion free, the tip of the newly exposed spur may bleed slightly. A blood-stopping agent should be applied to the tip of the spur if that should happen. If the outer portion of the spur does not twist free without too much force being exerted, the effort should not continue. Some roosters seem to have spurs almost of steel, too much force could break the leg. Another option is for the end of the spur to be slowly sanded away with a fine grit sand paper or nail file. This is quite a lengthy procedure and can take possibly a few days, working short periods at a time, but the method is safer than any other.

A less tedious practice is feather grooming, which male Onagadori in particular require from time to time. It is a procedure that they seem to enjoy, and they will usually set quite still for as long as is required of them.

Untangling the tail and saddle feathers can be time consuming if the bird manages to get them in a mess. Kept in a tomebako, the bird cannot easily do this. This problem is more likely to happen while he is out for exercise, if the tail is not held up by the handler.

The feathers infrequently need cleaning and should not be washed more than necessary as this destroys their integrity making them less durable. Tepid water with a mild detergent is the best thing to use if tail and saddle feathers do require washing. They should be handled carefully, old feathers especially may be brittle. Feathers should be blow-dried on a low setting in the direction of the barbs, never against the direction of the barbs, which would unlink the barbs and fray the feathers.

After blow-drying, the feathers can be lightly oiled with mineral oil, which is non-toxic. A bird cannot produce enough oil on its own to oil a very long tail. Nor can it reach along the length of the feathers to oil them properly as can a short tailed bird. The mineral oil can be applied with a clean soft cloth or paper towel, and will help to keep the feathers from becoming too brittle. Only a light application is required, care must be taken that the feathers do not become saturated, which can cause matting.

Dry skin may also become an issue, but it is not a serious problem and is easily treated. Whether on the comb, wattles, face, legs, or anywhere else, if the skin is dry, mineral oil can be used to moisten it. Only very occasional light applications should be made to sensitive head areas, as it could result in clogged pores. Legs and feet can be given heavier and more frequent treatments, as they are not as easily over-oiled.

Diagnosing Minor and Common Illnesses

This chapter is not meant to worry breeders, but rather to educate them regarding common problems that may occur, so that the effects can be minimized. The key is early detection, knowing the cause, knowing the treatment, and knowing when to cull, or not use the bird for breeding. This list is by no means a substitute for consulting a professional avian veterinarian or a book specifically on poultry health. It is meant to assist the breeder to know when a problem is serious enough to seek professional help and what to do when immediate care is needed.

During any disease outbreak, the affected individuals must be isolated at the first sign of illness, being kept as far from other birds as possible. When doing chores, sick birds should always be attended to last, after which hands should immediately be washed and sanitized. The sanitizing of all equipment, shoes, boots, and other clothing, is also necessary after each visit to any area containing ill birds. A keeper must not walk into an uninfected area with the same shoes and clothing worn to the quarantine area, without these items being sanitized first. Specific watering buckets and other equipment may be designated for quarantine areas and used in those areas exclusively in order not to spread any infection to unaffected areas of the poultry facility. A sanitizing liquid can be made by mixing bleach with water at the rate of ten percent bleach to ninety percent water.

Whenever acquiring new stock, they should be treated as if they are carrying disease and quarantined from the rest of the flock for a minimum of thirty days, as a precaution.

• Coccidiosis must be the most common ailment. It frequently occurs in young that become stressed by too cool a temperature or too damp an environment. It is caused by tiny parasites called protozoa, which infect the intestinal tract. Medicated chick starter is formulated to prevent this illness, but unfortunately it is still possible for them to be affected, as it does not kill the parasite, just keeps it in an encapsulated state.

Diagnosing cocci is not difficult. Affected birds will set around with feathers fluffed and acting chilled, and since it affects the digestive system, signs are also in the droppings which can be runny like diarrhea to thick and dark like tar, almost anything but normal, and usually with blood apparent due to the irritation of the digestive tract. Cocci is something that all chickens carry, but it remains dormant unless the bird becomes stressed. Stress, which taxes the immune system, can occur in many ways - any change to regular routines, changes in feed, changes in temperature or humidity, new pen mates, anything different; and most illnesses follow a period of stress. Cocci is usually not serious if caught in the early stages. It is treatable with a water-soluble medication called a coccidiostat, sold under several brand names. Unlike the medicated chick starter, a coccidiostat kills the parasite. Chicks that are raised within a flock are seldom affected, as low-grade exposure through other birds in the flock helps to build the offspring's resistance to the illness.

• CRD - Chronic Respiratory Disease, as the name implies, affects the respiratory organs of the bird. It is caused by *Mycoplasma gallisepticum*, a bacteria-like organism. (Acute respiratory disorders like Newcastle disease or infectious bronchitis can trigger this illness.) CRD will produce symptoms of coughing, sneezing, and nasal discharge (mucus from the nostrils). This can be accompanied by listlessness, low food intake, and loss of body weight. Broad-spectrum antibiotics can be used to treat this with varying success. The avian health / medication advisor at a local farm store carrying medications can advise on appropriate treatments.

• Infectious Bronchitis is characterized by symptoms of coughing, gasping, sneezing, and an abnormal rattling sound to the breathing. This virus affects only poultry and is not the same bronchitis virus that can be contracted by humans. It is considered the most contagious of all poultry diseases and can transmit through the air as well as on clothing and any objects in the coop. However, the virus is not transmitted through eggs, is easily killed by heat and common disinfectants, and will not live past one week in the building if poultry are not present. Immunization treatments are available, but must contain the local strain of the virus to be effective. They may be administered via the eyes or nostrils, or may be misted through the air for the birds to inhale, but are only effective if administered prior to the outbreak of the illness.

• Infectious Synovitis (*Mycoplasma synoviae*) is the inflammation of the synovial membrane lining the joints, and usually appears after a period of stress. Symptoms include swollen joints and foot pads, which in turn cause a stiff and arthritic-like walking motion. (For this reason the illness is also called Infectious Arthritis.) Wings and other joints can be affected in later stages. Respiratory symptoms such as nasal discharge or wheezing may also occur, as can decreased egg production. The disease can be confirmed by a blood test, which must be undertaken by someone licensed by the state. It is highly contagious and can be transmitted from bird to bird over great distances through the air, or can be carried by dust or on objects; nearly every exhibition and yard bird carries some type of a mycoplasma. Since it is most often transmitted by wild birds, poultry would have to be kept in a completely sterile environment not to contract it. Heavy doses of broad-spectrum antibiotics are the only treatment, but recovered birds still remain carriers and transmitters. The key to its control is to cull birds that exhibit symptoms.

• Marek's Disease is caused by a herpes virus and sadly has no treatment. It can be introduced through eggs and infected live birds, but even poultry products such as meat and feathers can carry the disease, although heat treatment can inactivate the virus on objects. Symptoms include paralysis, wasting away, dehydration, loss of appetite, pale face and comb, or sometimes death without any of the previous signs. Some birds seem immune; one bird in a pen may become infected while the others remain healthy. On another occasion an entire flock may come down with it. So if there is a definite diagnosis, the ill bird should be destroyed immediately to spare suffering and prevent transmission to other flock members, and pens should be cleaned and sanitized at once. Vaccines are available, but are only effective if administered prior to the outbreak of the illness.

• Neurological problems come in a variety of forms, develop in different ways, and have various different names. Most are not transmissible. Some are caused by a defect in the bird's development - aside of course from Marek's. Symptoms of neurological problems usually start as unusual neck movements, contorting, upside-down head twisting, and odd walking behavior. In stock of good breeding this is no more prevalent that any other common cause of mortality, perhaps even less so.

It has been reported that in some breeds, like the Silkie, such problems can be caused by a vitamin E deficiency and may be treatable by large doses of that vitamin in an oil form. If the feed already has a good balance of vitamins, it could be that the particular individual may be unable to absorb the nutrients properly. In this case, it may not be a desirable breeding candidate. It should be noted that if any bird is suspected of being unable to absorb Vitamin E, a deficiency in selenium could possibly be the cause. Many grains are deficient in this mineral, which is necessary for the proper absorption of vitamin E.

The progression of symptoms in neurological disorders can vary in speed, but it usually happens rapidly, no matter what the underlying cause.

One form of neurological problem is often called 'star gazing', the head and neck being raised straight up as if gazing at the stars. This is an involuntary movement that the bird is unable to control, and can be a symptom of several different diseases. Some of the causes could be: paramyxovirus, a viral infection affecting the neurological and respiratory systems; Meningitis, a bacterial infection causing a septic infection that can leak through the brain's blood barrier resulting in blood gathering around the brain; or major internal organ dysfunction disrupting the bird's usual metabolism. Environmental or chemical causes cannot be ruled out either. Substances such as cleaning chemicals, pesticides (pest strips, flea spray, etc), and herbicides can cause neurological disorders that can also result in the symptom of star gazing, as can extreme fluctuations in temperature or head trauma. Diagnosing the true cause of the symptom usually requires extensive testing by an avian health professional. If the symptom is the result of disease rather than environment, the bird should not be used for breeding as the tendency for low disease / infection resistance can be hereditary.

• Orthopedic disorders can affect any part of the skeleton. The most common problem is crooked toes on chicks, which can often be the result of an incubator being too hot at some point during incubation. Crooked toes on chicks can usually be straightened in a few days if taped into proper position with surgical tape soon after hatching. See more on the skeletal anatomy in the Anatomy chapter.

• Parasites such as worms, lice, and mites can quickly take their toll on a bird of almost any age once the pests find an acceptable host. Symptoms include weight loss, sunken-in or hollowed breast, gasping, lack of shine to the feathers, and a pale look of anemia.

Worms can be treated by proprietary poultry de-wormers, given in the dose as directed on the label.

Signs of lice and mites include loss of body weight, lack of shine to the feathers, and they may be visible on or around the skin of the vent. A white powdery build-up may also be present around the vent. Lice and mite treatments are usually in the form of a topical powder in which the birds can dust bathe, or a spray available for pigeons that can be sprayed directly onto the bird. Round 'mite protectors' available at pet shops for cage birds also work for males in tomebako. They should be hung on the inside of the tomebako, out of the bird's reach, following the directions as for a large cage bird. For birds able to dust bathe, grated citrus peels mixed into the litter may provide some benefit for some external parasites.

• Poisoning can have a few common possible causes: moldy feed, poisoned mouse droppings, or chemical poisoning such as that from herbicides or insecticides. Most toxins work quickly within the body and a postmortem is usually the only way to reveal the cause.

Mold poisoning, a form of Mycotoxicosis, can kill birds quickly. Mold can grow in feed very quickly during hot and humid conditions, so it is best kept in a re-sealable, airtight container with a sealing rubber gasket in order to prevent this problem. The most toxic forms of mold are invisible to the naked eye and possess no noticeable odor. These small amounts may not be visible, but are still lethal. Buying fresh custom mixed feed in no greater quantity than is usable within a thirty to sixty day period is always best, and feed should be carefully inspected after purchase and before feeding. Symptoms of mold ingestion are sores that resemble blisters in the mouth. It may also cause crop mycosis, indicated by extreme nervousness and feather picking.

The problem is similar to a yeast infection and may be treated with copper sulfate. Activated charcoal mixed with the feed may help to absorb toxins within the bodies of those fowl that have already ingested the toxin, but are not yet showing symptoms.

Rodent poisons usually contain an anticoagulant such as Warfarin or Brodifacoum. These chemicals work by thinning the blood, causing fatal internal bleeding. One mouse dropping can contain a lethal dose of some chemicals. Visible external signs of rodenticide poisoning include depression, anemia, reduced food intake, weakness, pale skin around the areas of the eyes and the mouth, and colic. Vitamin K1 is an effective treatment if administered soon after ingestion of the toxin. An avian health provider or other appropriate official should be consulted regarding dosage or to provide a prescription for medication if required. Injections with a small gauge needle, in several locations on the body to avoid hemorrhage, is the first step in treating such poisonings. After the first day of treatment, the oral version of the vitamin may be administered. Other K vitamins, including K3, are not effective in treating rodenticide poisoning.

Chemical herbicides and insecticides are extremely toxic and should never be used near poultry or their food and water source. If contamination of stock does occur, activated charcoal should be fed immediately upon detection. If the bird was actually observed ingesting something toxic and no longer than a few minutes has elapsed for it to be absorbed into the bird's body, vomiting can be induced with syrup of ipecac, and activated charcoal fed afterwards.

Anatomy

Caring for birds involves knowing about their anatomy - knowing how they should look and what is normal. Avian veterinarians may not always be available.

Since these birds involve so much in both time and resources, it is important to have as much knowledge as possible, in order to notice immediately when something is wrong, and to be able do whatever is possible with treatable problems.

The anatomy of long tailed fowl does not differ from that of most other chickens. It is important to know the basic characteristics of this anatomy, to know how a bird should look and feel.

This can aid the breeder in distinguishing a well-built bird from one that may be of lesser quality. It can also help to determine if, where, or how badly, a bird is injured.

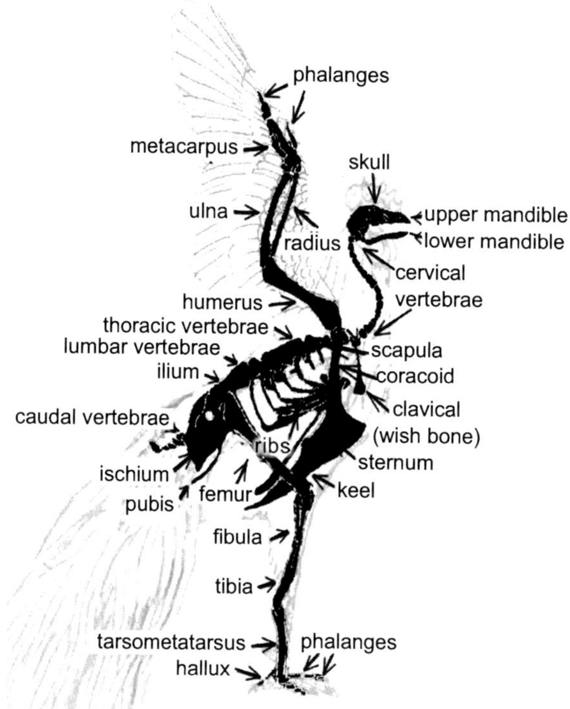

Left - A diagram of the skeletal anatomy of a male Onagadori. It is the same as that of most other domestic chickens.(Asian Game are slightly different.)

The skeletal anatomy should be strong and well built without any crooked or deformed bones.

Birds with crooked legs or crooked breastbones should particularly be avoided for use in breeding.

If a bird is injured in some way, understanding the correct skeletal form can help determine whether or not professional treatment is needed.

In the event of an injury, breaks are usually easily identified in bones that are not heavily covered with flesh and muscle, such as the extremities of the legs and wings or the lower portion of the breastbone. Swelling usually accompanies broken bones.

The breeder should decide when to consult an avian veterinarian, or when other options may be more practical, depending upon the symptoms and the extent of the injury.

The anatomy of the internal organs is more complex. More often an illness is the result of something wrong with an organ, rather than as a result of a skeletal injury. Each organ must work properly in cooperation with every other organ for optimal health.

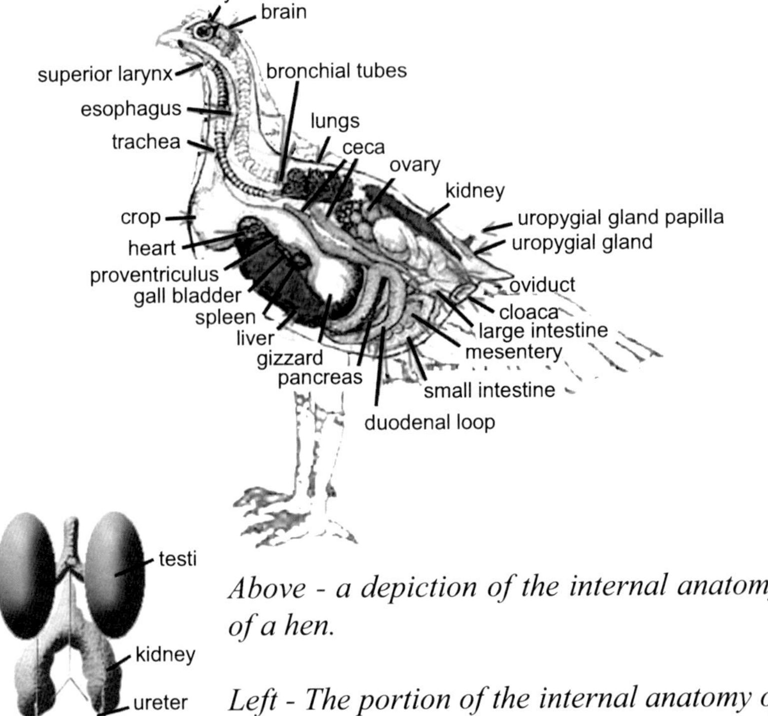

Above - a depiction of the internal anatomy of a hen.

Left - The portion of the internal anatomy of a rooster differing from that of a hen. The male anatomy is less complex than that of the female.

It is important that the proper coloration and texture of each organ is known. Having such knowledge will help in carrying out postmortem examinations to determine the cause of death, if a situation arises in which such a procedure is required. Classes in avian health can be taken with an avian health professional.

Onagadori and Phoenix feathers differ from each other. While both have a normal barb and hook feather structure, the texture of Onagadori feathers is soft and wispy, while those of Phoenix are more rigid. The actual physical differences are easily seen under a microscope.

Both microscopically viewed examples below are average breast feathers, the portion seen being mid-way between quill and tip. The Onagadori feather is of slightly greater thickness, needed to make the softer feathers stronger.

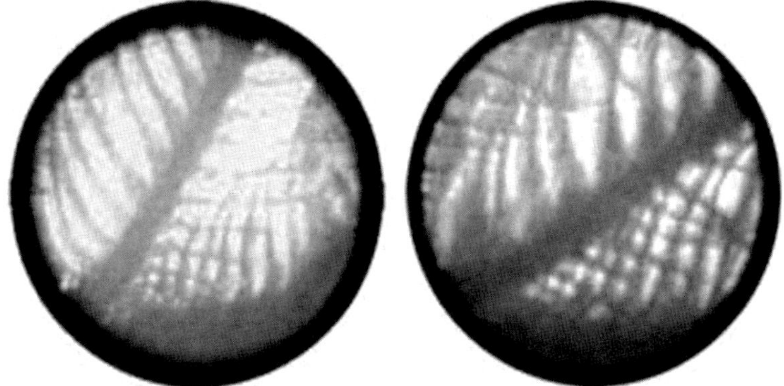

Above left - A feather from an Ismer Phoenix.
Above right - A feather from a modern Onagadori.

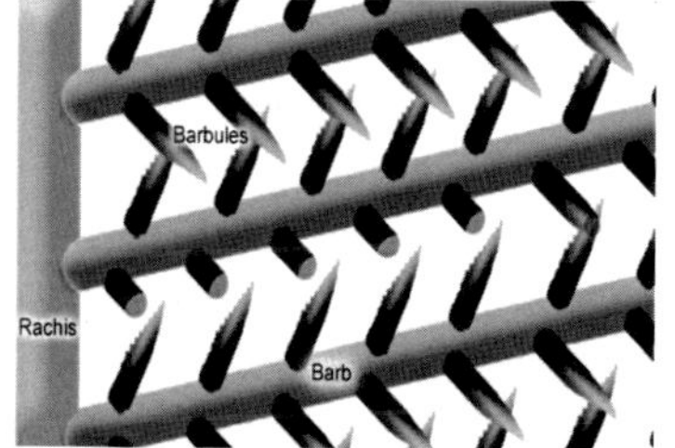

Phoenix *Onagadori*

Above - An artist's impression of the microscopic view, slightly exaggerated to illustrate the differences in the quantity and length of the barbs and barbules of the two feathers.

Left - A back feather from an Ismer Phoenix. The hair-like portion of the feather is shorter than that of the Onagadori feather shown at left. This feather type is a compromise between fine texture and durability. It has a fine look, but is sturdier than that of the Onagadori. Such feathers stay in better condition while the Phoenix is on the ground.

Left - A feather from between the shoulders of a young male Onagadori showing the typical fine hair-like lacing and distinct structure that is longer than the hair-like portion of the Phoenix feather above. Onagadori feathers overlap in such a way that the plumage on the back seems to be made up entirely of the hair-like feathering.

This type of feathering is delicate and only meets the needs of a highly pampered bird, carefully cared for in a tomebako and never left to run on the ground.

The feathering is ultimately what has captured not only the interest of poultry breeders but of all those who see long tailed fowl.

It is surely certain that for as long as dedicated breeders remain, these fowl will continue to stimulate a sense of wonder in all who view them, such is their mysterious beauty and the unique genetic sequence that produces it.

The rooster pictured at left and the pair of fowl pictured below are young Onagadori nearly two years of age. They are descendants of the Anton Huijkmann line and were raised by Marc King in the early 1990s.

The two Onagadori roosters pictured below are from a German line that Marc King visited in 1999.

The black-breasted red Ohiki rooster picture below is from the Astin line.

Glossary of Poultry Terms

Bantam - a term applying to dwarf chickens that often weigh no more than two pounds when fully grown, and are often miniature versions of large fowl.

Barbs - (also known as rami - plural, ramus - singular) are the hair-like parts of the feather that make up most of its surface. They point outward from the shaft and slightly back towards the tip of the feather, away from the follicle.

Barbules - (also known as radii - plural, radius - singular) extend outwards from both sides of the individual barbs. They are what hook each barb to the next. It is this linking together that gives a flight feather its flat surface to catch the air. When birds preen their feathers, they are re-linking the separated barbules to recondition the feather.

Blood Feather - a feather having blood in the quill to nourish the growth of the feather. The color of the quill (calamus) of a blood feather will be a dark bluish purple. Once a feather ceases to grow, and no longer requires a blood supply, the quill turns white and shrinks in diameter. The majority of the tail and saddle feathers of a modern Onagadori never cease to grow, thus never go out of blood feather.

Breeding Chart(s) - a record of all matings, hatches, and offspring, including notes regarding the health and quality of every bird.

Breeding Ration - a diet fed to adult birds when being bred. It contains a higher percentage of protein than other diets, which helps to increase fertility.

Candling - the process of checking whether or not an egg is fertile by placing it in front of a small bright light to view the silhouette of the developing embryo if present.

Cloaca (Vent) - the common orifice or outlet shared by the intestinal, urinary, and reproductive tracts of vertebrates such as reptiles, fish, and birds.

Cockerel - a male chicken under one year of age.

Codominant Genes - genes that react with others relevant to the same area of development to produce an average result in the offspring. A parent with a long tail bred to a short tail parent will produce offspring with tails shorter than the long tailed parent, but longer than the short tailed parent.

Comb - the (usually) red fleshy outgrowth on the top of a chicken's head.

Coop - the building in which poultry is kept.

Coverts - the feathers on the sides of the tail covering the main balance feathers. They are pointed at the end on a rooster, and rounded on a hen.

Crissum - the triangular group of feathers under the main tail feathers and above the vent. Also referred to as "under-tail coverts."

Cull - to remove and kill an ill bird or one of lesser quality. This must be carried out quickly and humanely.

Cushion - the female equivalent to the male's saddle.

Dominant Genes - these are genetic traits that are expressed or visible, in birds carrying them.

Duckwing - this is not a breed, but a variation of wild-type color pattern. It gets its name from the colored bar across the middle of the wing of the rooster, which looks similar to that on some ducks. The female corresponding to the duckwing male has a salmon colored breast. There are silver duckwing and gold duckwing varieties. The red version of this color pattern is more commonly known as black-breasted red or BBR, and is the coloration of the wild Red Jungle Fowl (*Gallus gallus*).

Expression / Expressed - visible characteristics of genes or combination of genes.

F1, F2, etc. - and F successions. F stands for filial, which is a term used to represent both male and female offspring. Generation one is F1. Generation two is F2, and so on.

Galliforme - order / classification of domestic chickens and wild Jungle Fowl. See Jungle Fowl.

Gluten - a specific type of protein formed in various grains when water is added and two proteins, glutanin and gliadin, combine. Any moisture added directly to the grain, or liquids within the body mixing with the grain, will cause the combination of these proteins and the formation of gluten. Some grains contain lesser quantities of these proteins than others.

Hackles - the finely textured cape of feathers around the bird's neck. The term is also used for the saddle feathers that drape over the lower portion of the back.

Hen - a female chicken over one year of age.

Heterozygosity / Heterozygous - the genetic state of carrying only one copy of a trait in the DNA, or of being impure; not producing offspring like itself when bred to another of the same breed. Example: Gt/gt+ i.e. carrying two different genes relevant to the same area of development.

Homozygosity / Homozygous - the state of possessing two identical copies of a trait in the DNA, or of being pure; producing offspring like itself when bred to another of the same breed. Example: Gt/Gt i.e. carrying two copies of one gene relevant to the same area of development.

Jungle Fowl - the wild ancestor to all domestic chickens, belonging to the same family as pheasants. There are four kinds of

Jungle Fowl: Ceylon (*Gallus lafayetii*), Green (*Gallus varius*), Gray (*Gallus sonneratii*), and Red (*Gallus gallus*). They once inhabited most of south-east Asia and China, but wild populations have now dwindled and many bloodlines are contaminated by that of feral domestic chickens. The Red Jungle Fowl is at least the partial ancestor of most domestic chickens; thus the domestic chicken is classified as -
Kingdom: *Animalia*. Phylum: *Chordata*. Class: *Aves*. Order: *Galliformes*. Family: *Phasianidae*. Genus: *Gallus*. Species: *gallus*. Subspecies: *domesticus*.

Large Fowl - a full sized chicken, usually weighing from around four to eight pounds or more when fully grown.

Line - a specific bloodline within a breed, being from particular parents or from a certain breeder.

Mandibles - the two halves, upper and lower, of a chicken's beak.

Maintenance Ration - a diet fed to adult birds when not being bred.

Main Tail Feathers (Retrices) - the flight feathers of the tail that act as a rudder to aid the bird in balance or flight. They are the straight stiff feathers under the coverts and above the crissum.

Minohiki - a long tailed breed of large fowl native to Japan, with exceptionally long saddle hackle feathers that drag along the ground. It has a normal annual molting pattern in all feather groups aside from the saddle hackles, which molt once every two years.

Molt - the yearly process most chickens go through in order to change their plumage. Old feathers are lost and new ones grow in their place.

Nagaodori - the name of Japanese long tailed fowl prior to 1920. At the time of their refinement the syllables changed order.

Nagaodori were heterozygous for the feather growth and non-molting traits. Modern Onagadori were developed from Nagaodori. In some cases, long-time breeders in Japan still refer to the breed as Nagaodori.

Neck Hackles - the feathers that start at the base of the head and extend down the neck and down to, or over, the shoulders.

Ohiki - a breed of bantam long tailed fowl native to Japan. A key feature of the breed is a trait that causes the legs to be very short in length. The short stature and a broad, round body are the two main characteristics that set it apart from bantam Phoenix.

Oil Gland (Uropygial gland) - located above the tail and below the group of feathers known as the saddle hackles, or saddles. It lies beneath the small, upright, fleshy structure known as the papilla. The gland secretes a natural conditioning oil through the papilla. A bird may be seen rubbing the papilla while preening; it will then spread this oil over its feathers to condition them.

Onagadori, modern - the modern Onagadori is the refined version of the breed as it exists after 1920. Being homozygous for the feather growth and non-molting traits, male Onagadori, unlike Phoenix, do not molt most of their tail feathers after acquiring their adult plumage, if cared for properly.

Onagadori, proto - A term developed by Marc King of www.casarocca.com to describe the forerunner of the modern bird i.e. the "Nagaodori" of the era prior to 1920. At the time of their refinement the syllables changed order. Proto is a Latin prefix meaning "that which gave rise to." "Proto" Onagadori were heterozygous for the feather growth and non-molting traits. Modern Onagadori were developed from these "protos" or Nagaodori.

Pecking Order - is the hierarchy and social structure of birds within the flock, enforced by the dominant fowl of the flock. Birds within a flock are not equals, there are both dominant males and dominant females. Dominant males are dominant over females and other males. Dominant females are usually only dominant over other females.

Phoenix - a standardized breed developed in the nineteenth century from crosses of Japanese long tailed breeds, Modern Game, and Leghorn. Unlike Onagadori, the male Phoenix molt their tail plumage regularly. Phoenix are bred in both bantam and large fowl sizes.

Pin Feather - the newly developing feather after molt.

Pip - the first tiny hole made in the egg shell by the hatching chick.

Postmortem - means 'after death', but usually refers to the after-death examination of the body and internal organs. To a trained eye it can help to expose the cause of death. It is also known as an autopsy or necropsy.

Preen - to preen, or preening: the act of the bird cleaning itself and reconditioning its feathers.

Pullet - a female chicken under one year of age.

Quill (Calamus) - the portion of the feather that is inside the skin follicle. It is tube-like, transparent, and hollow. No barbs are attached to the quill.

Recessive Genes - Recessive traits that require a copy from each parent to reproduce that trait in the offspring.

Recessive White - a recessive coloration trait in which all the bird's plumage is white. White Onagadori should have yellow legs, while white Phoenix have slate colored legs. Birds of this color should not be confused with albinos, which lack pigment altogether. It is merely a recessive gene causing the masking of the bird's true color, which is often silver duckwing, but can be nearly any color from the bird's recent ancestry.

Resistance - immunity to various illnesses.

Rooster / Cock - a male chicken over one year of age.

Saddles / Saddle Hackles - the long, thin, pointed feathers that start low on the back and reach down towards the base of the tail, parting in the middle and hanging down each side of the body.

Shaft (Rachis) - the portion of the feather, above the quill, to which the barbs are attached.

Shokoku - a large fowl long tailed breed from Japan. The breed has a duckwing coloration, red ear lobes and yellow legs.

Sickles - central pair of long curved feathers on the upward side of the tail.

Spur - the modified toe-nail type structure set on the back of the shank above the foot; most pronounced in males, but also present in many good quality long tailed females.

Starter - a feed ration for chicks, usually available as crumbles, or small crumbs, of food. It often contains a coccidiostat: a medication designed to prevent coccidiosis.

Tomebako - the wooden upright box in which the Nagaodori was developed, and in which a modern Onagadori rooster should be kept. A tomebako should be used only if the keeper can spend a great deal of time with the bird. A high degree of animal husbandry must be practiced with this method of rearing, and several long daily walks and good nutrition are vital.

Totenko - a black-breasted red large fowl long tailed chicken breed native to Japan. It characteristically has a long tail of two to three feet in length, but its defining quality is its long, melodious crow.

Trait - a physical characteristic caused by the expression of a gene or a combination of genes. Hidden traits are genes that a bird may possess, but are not expressed.

Vent - see Cloaca.

Wattles - the (usually) red fleshy outgrowths under the lower mandible of a chicken.

Yokohama - A long tailed breed developed in Europe from various Japanese long tailed breeds exported from Port Yokohama in Japan as early as the end of the nineteenth century.

Yolk Sac - the structure inside the egg, containing the yolk. During incubation, this sac is connected to the chick by a series of blood vessels and an umbilical cord. The chick feeds on the yolk as it develops inside the egg and it is absorbed into the chick's abdomen just before hatching. It continues to feed on the yolk for 24 hours after hatching.

Acknowledgements and Thanks

The information in these pages has been both acquired through research and accumulated through experience. The individuals who have helped in the research regarding these breeds also deserve credit and thanks for their work.

I thank the Lord for bringing me these wonderful birds. My mother first brought me home four or five blue and orange chicks for Easter. I was hooked for life! At six years old I knew then that they were for me. Mom had a great love for all animals, and raised us in a Christian home.

I would like to thank Marc King (casarocca.com) of Italy, one of my best friends. He did all the leg work, red tape, testing, gas, etc. to get the import, Ohiki, Tomaru, Denizli, Ismer Phoenix, and Schubert Phoenix here. Thanks!

Also I would like to thank Brian Reeder (Avalon Farms) for the detailed histories of the birds on this site; Brian Shamblin, who took care of a lot of the running around, paperwork, etc.; Donald

Barger, Cye Hyde, Dave Hotta, Frank Holder, for all their help in one way or another. Also a few others: Jeff Hann, Rourk Hiland, Will Warner, Ron Nelson, but mostly my dear friend David Rogers. Thanks for brightening my life. Thanks and God bless.
Toni-Marie Astin

I have so many to thank for this bird hobby. Thank God for making such beautiful creatures and giving me the energy to care for them. God is good!

I also thank my family for putting up with my birds crowding the barn.

Many thanks to my Great Uncle Ron, who sparked my interest in long tailed fowl by telling me of the "Yokohamas" he had seen in Japan. By description, they must have been Onagadori, but sadly he passed away prior to me obtaining my first long tailed fowl.

Thank you so much to my good friend Marc King for all of his help and advice.

I would also like to thank my friends Charles V. Owens, Jr. and Cheryl Owens of Elkhart, Indiana, and Julia Keeling of the Isle of Man, British Isles, for putting me in touch with contacts in Japan.

Many special thanks to Mrs. Kubota and her daughter Mrs. Goto, of the Onagadori Center in Kochi, Japan, who show such great devotion and dedication in caring for the Onagadori there, and who have given so much helpful advice regarding the birds. It is an honor to be in contact with you both.

Thank you so much to my friend Yoko Kondo for all of your help.

Thank you also to Mitsuyoshi Tatematsu for contributing the Shokoku photo on page 15. You do beautiful work!

To Melinda, thank you for all of your advice on poultry health.

I also offer my gratitude to Glenda Heywood, editor of the late *National Poultry News* publication, for all her great help and information; also to PattiAnn Gordon, who is a good friend and a well-respected poultry breeder and researcher.

Such special thanks that words can never convey, to Toni-Marie Astin, co-author. She is the one who got me started in long tailed breeds and she is a great friend. Much of this book is a compilation of things learned from her. I am truly blessed to have her for a friend. Thank you Toni!
David Rogers

About the Authors

Toni-Marie Astin's extensive background in animal husbandry includes her long-time work with registered Chihuahuas, fancy guppies, Himalayan and Siamese cats, and dozens of breeds of chickens at her facility, Onagadori South Feather Farm. She has familiarized herself with genetics and how they work. She also held a position in the medical field until she retired from the profession.

Mrs. Astin's knowledge of genetics and skills as an animal breeder are renowned. Her reputation has earned her great respect and admiration in this field.

David Rogers has been around poultry for most of his life; first, around the meat and egg utility flocks of his parents, then later with his pure-bred stock of various breeds. He specializes in rare poultry breeds, kept at Megumi Aviary, his hobby farm.

His poultry breeding efforts focus around non-molting long tailed fowl. He also occasionally writes for various poultry related publications to promote high levels of animal husbandry and the keeping and preservation of long tailed fowl.

Appendix 1 - Tomebako Building Plans

Most importantly, read, understand, and follow all power tool directions, and always wear appropriate safety items. These plans are for constructing a tomebako of approximate traditional Japanese style, but results will vary depending upon the lumber and hardware chosen. The authors assume no responsibility for a tomebako built following these plans, or for any result of its use with long tailed fowl or in any other manner.

(A)

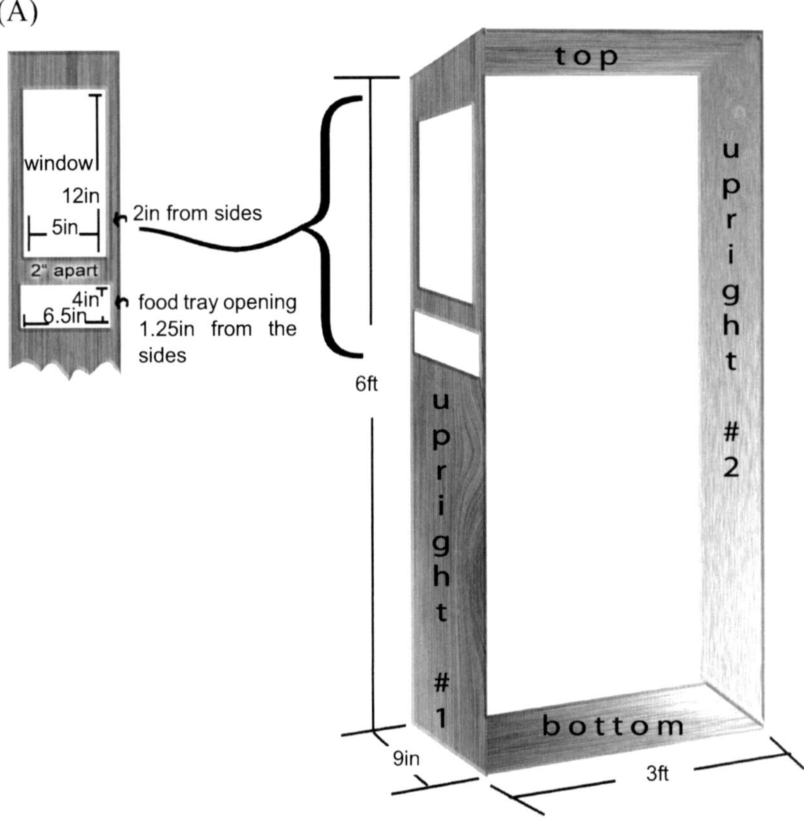

Construction begins with the outer shell of the tomebako. Pine is the suggested wood of choice. Avoid cedar and walnut.
Upright #1 and Upright #2 each measure 9in wide x 6ft high x .75in thick. They can be ripped from a 1in x 10in to the correct width on a table saw.

The Top and Bottom each measure 36in long x 9in wide x .75in thick. As with the Uprights, they can be ripped from a 1in x 10in to the correct width on a table saw.

The next step after cutting the four sides of the outer shell to size, is to cut holes in Upright #1 for the window and food tray opening.

Measure off the holes to the dimensions stated with a straight edge and / or square.

Then drill pilot holes in the inside corners of each intended opening. Be sure the holes are large enough to insert a jigsaw blade. Use the jigsaw to cut out and remove the wood from the window and food tray opening areas.

(B)

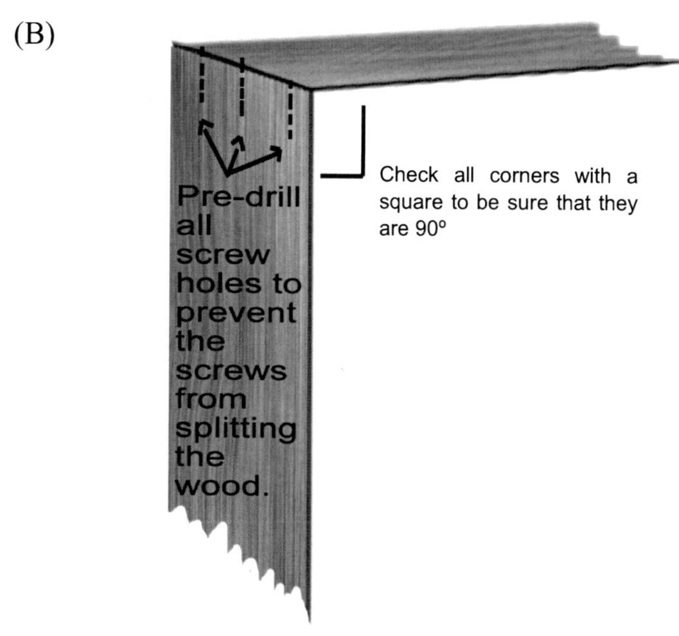

Fasten the Uprights to the Top and Bottom boards at 90º angles. The Uprights are fastened to the top side of the Bottom, and the Top then secures to the top side of the Uprights. Three 2in wood screws should be used at each corner. Pre-drill all holes through both pieces at each corner to prevent the screws from splitting the wood. Be sure to use the correct diameter drill bit for the screws being used.

Figure C - Cut two 2in x 2in boards to 49in in length. Drill a 1/4in diameter hole from front to back one inch from the top of each 2in x 2in board. Place them upright on the outer edges of the bottom board twenty-two inches from the left side of the Bottom board adjacent to Upright #1, and flush with the outside edges. Screw them onto the Bottom board with one screw each, first pre-drilling to prevent splitting.

Figure D - Cut a piece of wire long enough to stretch between the two 2in x 2in uprights and go through the holes and tie fast without causing the uprights to bow inward towards each other. Secure, trim, or file smooth any loose ends of this wire so that they do not pose a poking or cutting hazard. Rubber coated electrical wire could also be used. It is important that there are no sharp snags or burrs, as it is this on which the tail will rest.

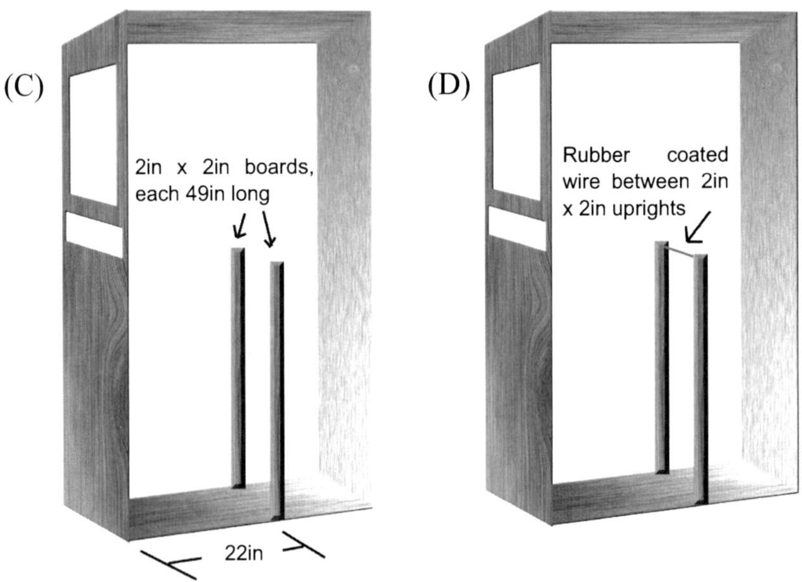

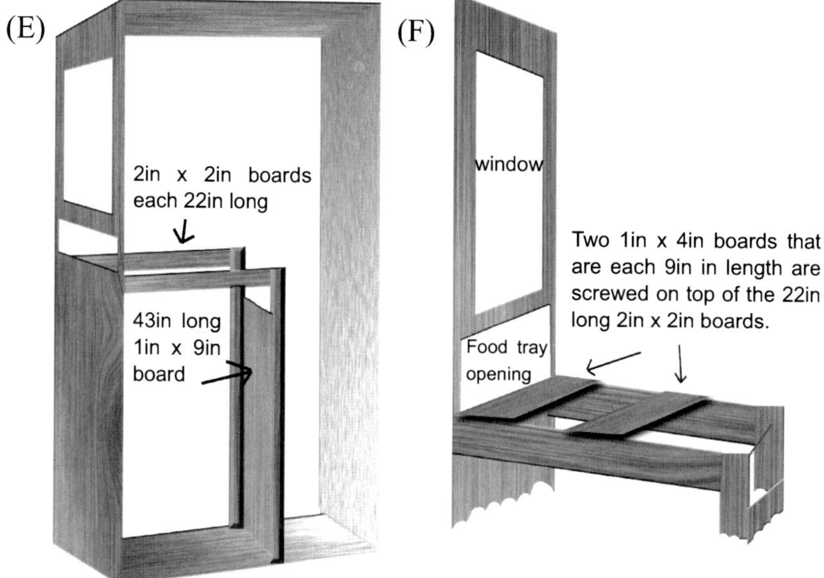

Figure E- The interior construction is further completed by cutting two 2in x 2in boards to twenty-two inches in length. Screw these into place between the 49in uprights, the interior side of Upright #1. They should be level from end to end and 1in below the food tray opening on the interior side of Upright #1. Another 1in x 9in board cut to forty-three inches in length should be screwed to the left side of the 2in x 2in uprights to form a barrier between the lower portions of the two sides of the tomebako. This will help to protect the tail, on the right, from the dropping tray on the left.

Figure F - Cut two lengths, each 9in long, from a 1in x 4in board. Screw the first board into place on top of the two 22in long 2in x 2in boards and against the interior side of Upright #1 just under the food tray opening. This board will serve as the food tray slide. The other length of 1in x 4in is the perch. If this tomebako is to be functional, the placement of the perch is critical. On average, for large fowl, there should be about four inches of space between the two 1in x 4in boards. This leaves about ten inches behind the perch for the droppings to fall. The perch may be covered with indoor / outdoor carpeting by wrapping a piece tightly around it so that it overlaps on the bottom side of the perch. Hold it in place with a large-headed screw through the overlapping section of carpeting at the bottom of the perch. It is a good idea to actually use the bird you intend to place in the tomebako to gauge an exact perch placement, which can vary depending upon the size of the bird: large fowl, bantam, or something in between.

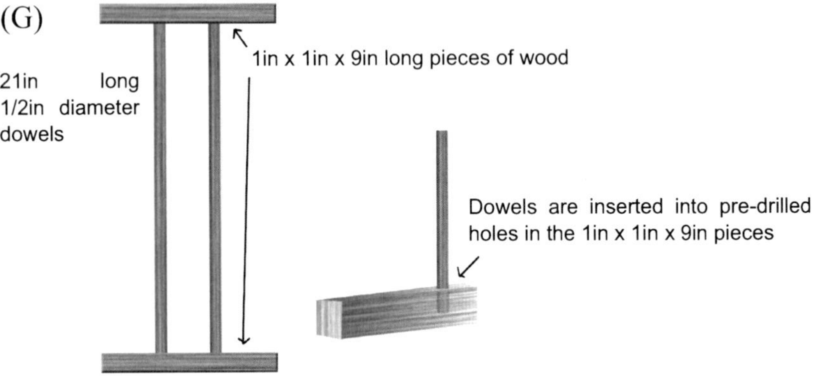

Figure G - 1/2in diameter dowels form the bars that keep the bird from making too much mess with its food in the container just in front of the perch. They are inserted into 1in x 1in x 9in long pieces of wood at the top and bottom of the bars. The entire assembly should measure 23in high x 9in wide; the length of the dowels will depend upon how far into the 1in x 1in pieces are inserted. The assembly may be held together with an indoor / outdoor wood glue.

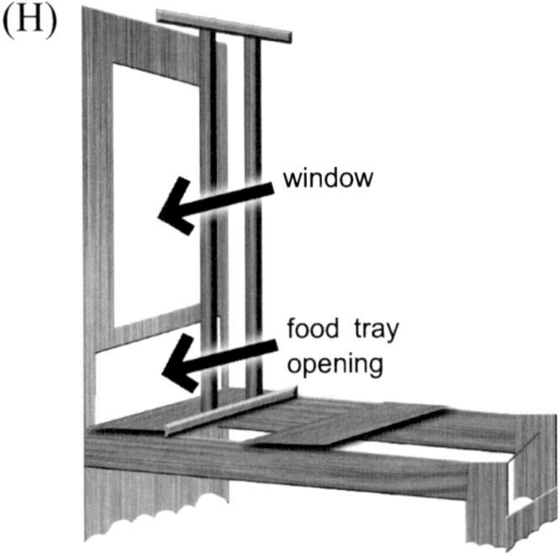

Figure H - This bar assembly is then screwed into place vertically on top of the 2in x 2in boards just behind the 1in x 4in that is the food tray slide, and reaching to the top of the tomebako. The 1in x 1in pieces should be pre-drilled before screwing them fast with the appropriately sized screw.

Figure I - The food tray is next to be built. Cut a piece of wood measuring 4in x 6in from .75in thick board. It should fit inside of the food tray opening in Upright #1. This will be the outward facing part of the food tray. A 2.5in x 6in piece of wood is used for the interior edge of the tray.

(I)

2.5in x 4.75in x .25in

These two pieces of .75in wood are held together with .25in thick plywood or luan. Brad nail with an air gun or glue with an indoor / outdoor wood glue the .25in thick sides to the 1in thick front and back. A bottom should then be made for this tray, but its dimensions may vary depending upon finished wood thicknesses. Cut it to size from 1in thick board so that it fits the inner area of the 1in thick and .25in thick sides. Brad nail it in place with an air gun or glue with an indoor / outdoor wood glue.

Choose any suitable handle to fix on the outside end of the food tray to make it easier to remove to fill with food.

The standard 6in long, 2-in-1 travel pet kennel food / water dish should just fit into this tray.

Now that the food tray has been made, what goes in must come out... bringing us to the dropping tray. This is no more than simply a box built in the same manner as the food tray, with finished dimensions being 20in long x 9in wide x 3in to 4in deep; or a plastic storage container could be used. This tray is set on the floor of the tomebako under the perch and food tray. It should be filled with fresh pine shavings or other litter and changed daily.

The back of the tomebako can be cut from plywood or luan. It is best to do the measuring for the back independently as the outside dimensions of the tomebako may vary depending upon exact lumber thickness. Measure the outside height and width of the tomebako, cut a piece of wood with these dimensions and secure it to the outside back of the tomebako along Upright #1, Upright #2, Top, and Bottom with brad nails and air gun, or with an outdoor grade wood glue.

(J)

There are three doors, two on the left side and one on the right. Door #1 is actually divided into two vertical halves. They are hinged together in the middle so that both halves fold outwards and to the left.

Door #2 is hinged in three places to fold outwards to the right.

Door #3 covers the dropping tray compartment. It also folds outwards to the left away from the center of the tomebako.

The doors can be made as ornate or plain as desired. They

should be measured to fit in the same way as was the back, meeting in the middle of the tomebako slightly off-center over the upright 2in x 2in at the front.

Frame each door with .75in thick stock that has been ripped to 2in wide. Each frame can be jointed at the corners either by a 90° angle or two 45° angles. Cover each door on the back of the frame with .25in plywood or luan.

Two inch hinges work well for hanging the doors. The handle may be a simple hook and eye style of latch, a turn-knob type, or any other suitable fixture.

The completed tomebako can be used as a piece of furniture or conversation piece in your home if built with furniture quality materials. If to be used for poultry, caution should be taken regarding choice of any stain or paint, being sure that it produces no fumes when dry. The food tray, perch, and dowels should never be treated. The outside of the window on Upright #1 can be covered with hardware cloth, dowel bars, or Plexiglas.

(K)

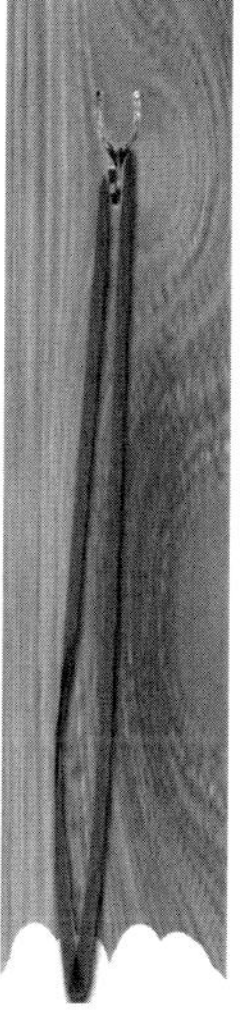

Figure K - A 40in long loop of silk ribbon, or other soft material, is hung from a metal hook screwed into the interior side of Upright #2, eight inches from the ceiling. This loop is used to keep the tail held back.

Left - The outside of a tomebako.

Above right - A young silver duckwing male, Rogers line, sets on his perch inside a tomebako. Below - Three individual stalls.

A full-spectrum florescent light on the ceiling of the tomebako may be used if enough light is not available to the bird through the window. Too bright lighting may cause some roosters to become aggressive; care must be taken to provide a suitable level.

As an alternative to keeping males in tomebako, individual stalls may be used. These stalls should measure approximately six feet square by eight feet in height.

Pine wood shavings scattered upon the floor 4in to 6in deep provide a protective bedding for the plumage while the bird is walking around on the floor.

Food and water dishes should be hung on the wall at one end of the high perch to eliminate some of the need for a bird to leave its perch. Birds raised in this way will prefer to stay perched.

Appendix 2 - Japanese Names and Words Explained

Kurokashiwa, 黒柏 (Kōō-rō-kä-shē-wä), is made up of the character for black, 黒 "Kōō-rō", and the character 柏 "kä-shē-wä" meaning oak. In Japan, various kinds of meat were formerly referred to by the meat's color. Flowers or autumn tree leaves of the corresponding colors were used as synonymous names for the meat. Boar meat, being bright pink, was referred to as "botan" or peony. Deer meat, being red, was "momiji" or maple. Chicken meat, being yellow, was called "kashiwa" or oak. Thus Kurokashiwa literally means "black chicken", alluding to the bird being black in color and having yellow meat, or simply just being a chicken.

Minohiki (-dori), 蓑曳鶏 (Mē-nō-hē-kē-dō-rē) - The first character 蓑 "mino" (mē-nō) is the word for the old-time Japanese straw raincoat. The kanji 曳 "hiki" (hē-kē) means to tow or drag. The kanji 鶏 "tori" (tō-rē) for fowl, takes on a dulled consonant when combined with another word and becomes "dori" (dō-rē). The "dori" is often dropped from the spoken word and is understood as implied. All together it literally means "raincoat dragging fowl". This name alludes to the resemblance that the dragging saddle feathers have to the garment.

Nagaodori, 長尾鶏 (Nä-gä-ō-dō-rē) is the former arrangement of the same syllables as in the word "Onagadori". See Onagadori.

Ohiki, 尾曳 (Ō-hē-kē), made up of the kanji 尾 "Ō" meaning "tail" and the kanji 曳 "hiki" (hē-kē), meaning to tow or drag. Thus "Ohiki" simply means "tail dragger".

Onagadori, 尾長鶏 (Ō-nä-gä-dō-rē) broken down into three words is: 尾 "Ō" meaning "tail", 長 "nä-gä" which is "long", and 鶏 "tori" (tō-rē) for "chicken" or "fowl". When placed with another word, "tori" takes on a dulled consonant and becomes "dori" (dō-rē). Onagadori literally means "long-tail fowl."

Shokoku, 小国 (Shō-kō-kōō), or rather the breed's ancestors, were brought to Japan from China when Japanese scholars were sent there to study the Chinese culture from the 7th through the 9th centuries AD. It is said to be native to a region in China known as 昌国 (read "Shokoku" in Japanese). At some point in history the kanji utilized changed to 小国. The character 小 "shō," means "small," and the character 国 "koku" (kō-ko͞o), means "country" or "nation". The The kanji 鶏 "tori" (tō-rē) for fowl, is sometimes added to the written word. It takes on a dulled consonant when combined with another word and becomes "dori" (dō-rē). The "dori" is often dropped from the spoken word and is understood as implied. So the name Shokoku refers to what was thought to be the original area of the breed's ancestors.

Tomebako, 止め箱 (tō-mĕ-bä-kō) - The first two characters are one word. The kanji 止 "tō" and the hiragana め "mĕ" are read together as "tome" (tō-mĕ), meaning "to stop". The next character is 箱 "hä-kō" meaning box. The kanji "hako" takes on a dulled consonant when placed with another word and is read as "bä-kō". Therefore "tomebako" means "stopping box", implying a box for stopping the molting process.

Totenko, 東天紅 (Tō-tĕn-kō), combines the characters for "east", "sky / the heavens", and "crimson". The first character 東 meaning "east" borrows the pronunciation "Tō" from the ancient form of the Chinese language. It can also be read as "higashi" in the native Japanese language. The next character, 天 "tĕn", means "sky / the heavens". The last character, 紅 "kō", meaning crimson also borrows its pronunciation from the ancient form of the Chinese language in this case. The character 紅 may also be read as "kurenai" in the native Japanese language.

In the word Totenko, "crimson" does not allude to the color of the fowl, but to the color of the sky. Totenko actually means "rooster call" or "voice heard when the sky becomes crimson in the east"; i.e. at the break of dawn.

Appendix 3 -
Probable Movement of the Ancestors of Long Tailed Breeds

•(1) This ancient trade route was used to trade spices and textiles between China and Java. Southern Asia is made up of groups of islands, and many of the inhabitants were seafaring fishermen and traders, regularly participating in trade with other islands.

•(2) Japanese scholars traveled back and forth from China during the 7th through 9th centuries AD. It is thought that the ancestors of the Shokoku originated in China and were introduced to Japan at that time.

•(3) Various long tailed breeds have been exported from Japan to Europe since the end of the nineteenth century.

Strength to go on

Taking care of the fowl and just life in general takes a lot out of us daily. Where do you draw your strength from? The Bible, God's living word, says the joy of the Lord is your strength. The joy of having a relationship with Jesus Christ gives strength and comfort.

Jesus Christ is a gift to us from our heavenly Father. John 3:16 says, "For God so loved the world, that he gave his only begotten Son, that whosoever believes on him should not perish, but have eternal life."

Having a personal relationship with our heavenly Father, the creator of the universe, through Jesus Christ is easy. Simply have faith and believe. The Bible verse Hebrews 11:6 says, "But without faith it is impossible to please God: for anyone who comes to God must believe that He is, and that He is a rewarder of them that diligently seek Him." The Bible verse Romans 10:9 says, "Because, if you confess with your mouth, "Jesus is Lord," and you believe in your heart that God raised Him from the dead, you will be saved."

This is the most important relationship we can have. Before we have that relationship: that empty spot we feel in our heart at times is this missing relationship we were created to have. God wants a relationship with us and accepts us with love and open arms.

Asking Christ into your life is simple: pray with sincerity, "Father God, please forgive me for not living for You. I believe and confess Your Son, Jesus Christ, is Lord. I believe that He died on the cross, shed His blood for me, and that You raised Him from the dead. I ask You Lord Jesus to come into my life and help me to live my life for God. Thank you for saving me. In Jesus' name, Amen."

Anyone who prays that prayer with sincerity is a new creation in Christ and has a relationship with Father God through Him.

Pray and ask God to guide and comfort you. Live each day praising the Lord in all you do.

Made in the USA
Middletown, DE
17 October 2023

40985302R00049